Unaccompanied Minors

Unaccompanied Minors

■ ■ ■

Immigrant Youth, School Choice, and the Pursuit of Equity

CAROLYN SATTIN-BAJAJ

Harvard Education Press
Cambridge, Massachusetts

Library of Congress Control Number 2014935205

Paperback ISBN 978-1-61250-709-5
Library Edition ISBN 978-1-61250-710-1

Published by Harvard Education Press,
an imprint of the Harvard Education Publishing Group

Harvard Education Press
8 Story Street
Cambridge, MA 02138

Cover Design: Joel Gendron
Cover Photo: Getty Images/Marilyn Nieves/Vetta
The typefaces used in this book are Sabon and Ocean Sans

CONTENTS

■ ■ ■

Immigration, Inequality, and School Choice Policy

THE POST-1965 WAVE of "new" immigration to the United States ushered in a series of profound demographic changes in American schools. Children of immigrants are now the fastest-growing segment of the school-age population in the United States. In 2010, 24 percent of children ages seventeen and under lived at home with at least one immigrant parent, and this figure is projected to reach 30 percent by 2018.[1] Nearly two-thirds of children of immigrants have origins in Latin America, and more than a quarter of them live in poverty.[2] The exponential growth in the size of the immigrant-origin student population in the United States has come at a time when earning at least a high school diploma has never been more important for long-term personal and professional stability. Whereas at the start of the twentieth century people with limited formal education were able to achieve some degree of mobility, education beyond high school has become a prerequisite for entry into most professional sectors of today's economy.[3] The need to provide high-quality educational opportunities to low-income,

immigrant-origin youth—particularly Latinos—has therefore emerged as a central issue in current conversations about education,
social cohesion, and national progress.

In the midst of these significant economic and global population shifts, income and educational inequality have been on the rise.
The income gap between the richest and poorest Americans is larger
today than at any other time in the last century.[4] Educational indicators paint a similarly grim portrait. Test score gaps between high-
and low-income students are widening, and there is large variation
in the quality of schools they attend. Significant differences also exist in educational attainment and college graduation rates by family
income, and longstanding racial/ethnic disparities in achievement
persist.[5] Results from the National Assessment of Educational Progress (NAEP) show that black and Latino students score far below
their white and Asian peers on literacy and mathematics proficiency,
and they also have lower high school graduation rates and are less
likely to complete college than white or Asian students.[6]

These educational patterns are raising alarm about ongoing
educational inequity and their ramifications. They also point to
schools' ineffectiveness in preparing all students for the twenty-
first century.[7] Given that over 60 percent of Latino students live
in immigrant-led households and 34 percent live in poverty, these
trends point to significant failures in integrating and educating
large numbers of low-income children of Latin American immigrants.[8] As a result, politicians, policy makers, and citizens alike
are increasingly focused on identifying solutions to both narrow
the gaps and remedy the troubling disparities in educational access
and attainment.

School choice features prominently among the policies being
implemented in districts across the country to address the well-
documented "opportunity gaps" in education. School choice com-
prises everything from charter schools (publicly funded schools
that usually operate outside of district administrative structures)
and magnet schools (public schools with distinctive, thematic cur-

ricula designed to attract students of diverse socioeconomic and racial/ethnic backgrounds), to inter- and intradistrict transfer programs and voucher plans (public funds given to parents to cover private school tuitions). While forms of school choice have been in place since the school desegregation movement of the 1960s, districts across the United States have adopted school choice with renewed vigor in recent years as part of a broader set of market-based educational reform strategies proposed to improve school quality while simultaneously increasing educational equity.

Today, forty-two states and the District of Columbia have charter school laws, and all but four states have some form of inter- or intradistrict open enrollment policy.[9] The federal government has also publicly endorsed school choice, most prominently through the federal Race to the Top grant competition that penalizes states without charter school laws in place and those that have caps on the number of charter schools allowed. Yet many claims by school choice proponents about its promise to increase educational equity and improve disadvantaged students' access to higher quality educational opportunities have yet to achieve a broad consensus of agreement among policy analysts and researchers.[10]

The pursuit of educational equity is one of a number of rationales used to support school choice policies. Arguments about the value of competition and the importance of parental control over education are also frequently invoked by school choice advocates. However, equity goals are at the forefront of many school districts' public statements justifying the adoption of these policies. *Unaccompanied Minors* takes on the question of the compatibility of school choice and educational equity goals through a case study of New York City's mandatory high school choice policy. It focuses specifically on four distinct actors in school choice—district administrators, school personnel, students, and parents. By examining their expectations, behaviors, perspectives, and experiences, the book identifies some of the underlying processes that contribute to students' and families' diverse forms of engagement in school choice and to the wide variation found in students' rates of admission to high-performing high schools. In doing so, it sheds light on the growing body of empirical evidence suggesting the limits of school choice policies—in New York and elsewhere—to facilitate disadvantaged students' access to better educational opportunities.[11]

I start from the premise that choice policies are not inevitably destined to perpetuate inequality. Rather, school choice may offer a path forward in combatting persistent educational stratification when carefully designed and implemented. The main argument advanced in this book is that school choice policies often rest on faulty normative assumptions about parental involvement, educational beliefs, and access to resources to inform decisions about schools. Drawing on a multiyear study of low-income Latino immigrant-origin students' and families' experiences with high school choice in New York City, the book presents data from observations of city-wide and school-based activities related to high school choice, document analysis, and interviews conducted with district administrators, school personnel, students, and parents that illustrate the extent to which the goals, assumptions, and ideas behind school choice policies in theory can deviate from what actually happens in practice. Middle school "IS 725,"* which approximates the type of middle schools that low-income, Latino immigrant-origin youth living in urban areas have been shown to attend in terms of size, student demographic makeup, and academic outcomes, served as a case study site.[12] A majority of observations took place at IS 725, and student and parent interview participants were recruited primarily from the school's eighth-grade population.

The school choice decision making of the low-income Latino youth from IS 725 provides evidence of the gap between the New York City Department of Education's imagined version of choice and the realities on the ground. These students' experiences with high school choice highlight three distinct areas of misalignment:

---

*All names of schools and people have been changed to preserve confidentiality.

the district's erroneous expectations of extensive parental involve-ment in high school searches and decision making; unrealistic ex-pectations of intensive student engagement in school search ac-tivities; and unfounded expectations of substantial school-based guidance. In the end, few of the low-income Latino students in the study were assigned to higher performing high schools than the failing neighborhood schools they would have attended without choice. In the following chapters, I explore and explain how the faulty assumptions undergirding the choice policy, a lack of over-sight of school-level activities, and limited resources dedicated to choice interacted with families' socioeconomic backgrounds, cul-tural values, and child-rearing practices in ways that ultimately contributed to the failure of the high school choice policy on this test of educational equity.

While the book isolates a series of barriers that impede the promotion of equity through choice in New York, it also considers the resources, practices, and behaviors that help some (typically higher income) students and families successfully obtain assign-ments in selective, high performing high schools within the choice marketplace. Many of the low-income eighth-grade children of Latin American immigrants were ill-equipped to make informed decisions about high schools, but this was not the case for all stu-dents and families. A comparative sample of higher income chil-dren of Asian immigrants enrolled at the case study middle school and upper-middle-class white parents of eighth-grade students at-tending different middle schools revealed some of the conditions under which the results of the high school choice process could be vastly different. When parents lived up to the New York City Department of Education's expectations of significant involvement in the process and when students actively engaged in school re-search and exploration, they were able to streamline the process and leverage knowledge, tools, and supports to produce favorable outcomes (in the form of desired, usually elite high school assign-ments). These findings were unsurprising given that the policy as-sumed typically middle-class parenting practices. At the same time, they drew attention to the specific resources, supports, behaviors, and activities that helped students (and parents) make thoughtful, deliberate school choices.[13]

In light of students' and families' diverse understandings, resources, and choice experiences in New York City and the ongoing challenges in progressing toward greater educational equity through choice, the book argues that school systems and schools must fundamentally rethink their roles and responsibilities. Rather than disconnected policy creators, information transmitters, and policy implementers, district leaders and school personnel must take on the task of educating students and families about policies and what is expected of them. They must ensure that all choice participants have access to the information and guidance they need to make knowledge-based decisions. Policies should also be designed or adapted to better reflect the range of parenting practices, philosophies, and resources represented among the families in the district.

A key finding is that students' development of effective research, analytic, and decision-making skills could be as important an outcome of participation in school choice programs as access to better educational options. Such skills are potentially applicable to a vast array of institutional, professional, and personal contexts. There are thus manifold possible benefits of school districts investing in efforts to help all choice participants understand how to make informed decisions and how to navigate institutions or complex bureaucratic processes.

Unaccompanied Minors includes a series of recommendations for actions that can be considered at the district, school, community, and individual family levels to increase the equity potential of school choice policies. These include broader changes to policy, reallocation of resources, and improved district- and school-level outreach and communication strategies as well as increased focused on community partnerships, student support, and family engagement efforts. A number of the suggestions advanced here are also focused on enlisting school-based resources to assist students and parents in generating invaluable research and decision-making tools. Such tools and skills can facilitate effective participation in school choice and a host of other policies and processes, not just in education. This book suggests a rethinking and expansion of the role of schools to include helping families understand how to negotiate different institutional relationships, environments, and experiences. Emphasizing the power and possibility of schools, it offers a path forward in the pursuit of access and equity.

WHY STUDY HIGH SCHOOL CHOICE IN NEW YORK CITY?

New York City is home to children living in some of the country's poorest neighborhoods and children of some of the highest paid, most educated people in the world. Its schools serve students from across the socioeconomic spectrum, and they have origins in nearly every country around the globe. Under New York City's mandatory high school choice policy, these children must compete for a scarce supply of seats in the city's few high performing high schools. The glaring differences that exist in their families' resources, educational backgrounds, and cultural models raise questions about whether school choice policies such as the one in place in New York City can facilitate the equitable distribution of high-quality educational opportunities among an ever more heterogeneous public school population. It therefore serves as a compelling site for exploration of the main questions driving this book. Lessons from New York City's school choice context about what is and is not working, why, and how to improve policies and practices to make educational equity a more reasonable goal have implications for a host of other districts attempting similar reforms.

As the largest urban school district in the United States with a total student enrollment greater than that of thirty-eight states, New York City has been at the center of innovative education policy reforms for decades. Under mayoral control for over a decade, the New York City Department of Education (NYCDOE) has been at the forefront of a national education reform movement. School districts nationwide have turned to New York City for ideas, strategies, and insights about how to combat educational inequity and promote achievement among all students. From the creation of hundreds of small schools to the development of a comprehensive school accountability program, NYCDOE has experimented with a variety of policies and strategies to improve results. School choice has been at the very heart of its efforts.

Nearly every large urban school district has considered and/or implemented some form of school choice policy over the last decade and a half, and many exurban and suburban districts have done the same. Moreover, a growing number of districts, including New York, Chicago, New Orleans, Philadelphia, and others, are embracing a "portfolio model" of schooling in which families are presented with a range of educational options (e.g., district public, charter, and virtual schools) and the central office serves as manager rather than direct operator of all schools. The policy recommendations provided at the end of the book could be readily adapted to the different educational, demographic, political, and geographic contexts that exist across the United States and even internationally.

The high school choice policy in New York City is also representative of public policies, social practices, and bureaucratic processes that take for granted possession of particular cultural models and values and/or implicitly demand certain institutional knowledge, skills, and resources. The proliferation of postsecondary educational institutions of extremely variable quality, for example, makes early development of research and analytical skills for informed college choice more vital than ever. As a result, arguments advanced in this book are relevant beyond New York City and generalizable to policies other than school choice.

OVERVIEW OF THE BOOK

The chapters that follow sketch a detailed picture of low-income Latino youth's experiences with compulsory high school choice in

New York City. In doing so, they elucidate the factors that jeopardize the equity potential of school choice policies and identify opportunities to improve them. First, the basic tenets of New York City's choice policy and the assumptions on which it is based are presented. These assumptions inform the district's implementation of the policy—including provision of support, resources, and oversight of school-based guidance to students and families. Next, my argument reveals the chasm between NYCDOE's imagined version of the choice policy—in terms of school-level support, student behaviors, and parental involvement—and the reality for low-income Latino eighth-grade students required to participate in it. Instances of alignment between district expectations and higher income parents' and students' engagement in choice provide a counterpoint that demonstrates the resources, supports, and behaviors necessary to effectively negotiate choice.

Chapter 1 introduces the high school choice policy and situates it within the larger history of school reform in New York City. It offers a brief description of the case-study middle school ("IS 725") and explains the rationale for its selection. Chapter 2 draws on school choice publications, ethnographic observations of city-wide high school choice events, and interviews with NYCDOE administrators to present district personnel's goals for the choice policy, their understanding of their and school personnel's roles and responsibilities in implementing the policy, and their ideas about how students and parents should effectively search for and select high schools. It also examines the form and content of the school choice information provided by NYCDOE. The chapter argues that even with its limited role in the choice process—confined simply to information provision—the district fell far short of meeting its constituents' most basic informational needs. Furthermore, issues of language and accessibility of school choice materials only exacerbated larger problems associated with the design and implementation of the choice policy: faulty assumptions about student engagement and parental involvement in high school choice and the district leadership's failure to articulate clear, enforceable expectations of school personnel's involvement in the choice process.

The chapter lays out the flawed foundation upon which New York City's imperfect school choice policy is based.

In chapter 3, ethnographic data from IS 725 paint a portrait of ground-level implementation of the high school choice policy. Guidance counselors' and school administrators' behaviors at IS 725 show the disparity between NYCDOE officials' ideas about implementation of the choice process in theory and what actually takes place in a school building. In the end, most students at IS 725 were left to navigate the vast universe of high school options with minimal school-based support and guidance. This chapter reveals some of the consequences of the lack of established mandates about school personnel's responsibilities to students and parents vis-à-vis high school choice. It argues that in the era of testing and accountability, schools logically organize themselves and distribute resources to meet the benchmarks for which they will be rewarded and pay less attention to policies for which they will not be judged. To be taken seriously by school administrators and staff, school choice policies must be matched with clearly articulated expectations of middle school actions, formal mechanisms for monitoring performance, and adequate resources to defray the associated costs of providing these support services.

In part 2, chapter 4 pivots to students' experiences with high school choice. It compares how different subgroups of students at IS 725 navigated choice by examining four separate factors in their school search and decision-making processes: the role of peers, school-based information sources, family members, and the school selection criteria used to make choices. The chapter highlights the contrast between the experiences of predominantly second-generation, Asian-origin, middle-class students in the school's gifted and talented track and three other groups of students: high performing first- and second-generation Latino students in the honors and regular tracks; low performing second- and third-generation Latino and African American students in the regular track; and recent immigrants from the Dominican Republic, Ecuador, and Mexico in the Spanish bilingual track.

The Asian-origin gifted and talented track students manifested a clear grasp of the policy and school offerings, conducted extensive research on schools, and enjoyed significant guidance from family members, peers, and school personnel. By contrast, the other students showed a very limited understanding of choice, lacked clear criteria for school selections, and chose high schools in relative isolation. These students' divergent approaches to high school choice and their final high school assignments expose some of the consequences of district administrators' inaccurate assumptions, parents' roles, school-based guidance, and students' school search activities.

Chapter 5 delves more deeply into the underlying processes and structural and cultural factors contributing to the variation in students' choice experiences. It defines the two categories used to classify students' approaches, *strategic choice* and *passive choice*, and elaborates the concepts of an *institutional compass* and a *multiply reinforced orientation*—critical components of strategic choice. The chapter explores the constituent elements of an institutional compass and a multiply reinforced orientation and describes the conditions under which these essential tools can be developed and used effectively to facilitate strategic choice. The chapter argues that building students' skills and sensibilities needed to engage in strategic choice can have payoffs far beyond the immediate school choice context given their applicability to a host of institutional environments and personal and professional experiences.

Chapter 6 takes up the role of parents. It draws on parent interviews to identify patterns of overlap and divergence between NYCDOE's expectations and parents' engagement in high school choice. The narratives of prototypical high-income, native-born white parents and low-income Latin American immigrant parents show their vastly different perspectives, knowledge, goals, and activities vis-à-vis high school choice. The chapter argues that despite a predominantly low-income and minority population being educated in New York City schools, the well-documented alignment between many education policies and white, middle-class norms applies to the case of high school choice in New York City as well. By demonstrating the extent to which low-income Latin American immigrant parents' views and behaviors depart from expectations, the chapter goes even further in questioning the underlying assumptions of New York City's policy and some of the basic theoretical underpinnings of school choice more generally.

The conclusion revisits the main arguments presented throughout the book and elaborates a series of policy and programmatic recommendations aimed to leverage the potential of school choice policies to promote equity and broader skill development. Many of the proposed policy changes advanced throughout the book emphasize the need for schools to take a more central role in direct instruction and guidance for families participating in choice. The conclusion reviews the recent move away from redistributive equity policies such as these in education to those geared toward "excellence for all," and discusses the study's findings and proposed policy changes in light of this shift.

The recommendations presented in the conclusion include improvements to school- and district-level practices to inform, instruct, and engage students in activities that help them understand, prepare for, and effectively engage in informed school choice. Increased training for school personnel, requirements for school-based outreach to students and families participating in choice, and incentives for schools to experiment with innovative ways to engage families comprise only some of the ideas advanced. The conclusion also suggests a range of policies, practices, and structures geared toward helping all students get access to the assets and resources that strategic choosers have at their disposal—an institutional compass and multiply reinforced orientation among them. These proposals focus explicitly on building structures, supports, and activities to promote the development of skills and strategies that can be honed through the process of choosing high schools in New York City—e.g., conducting research, analyzing school performance and other data, weighing options, and ranking preferences—but are in fact applicable beyond school choice. My conclusion echoes educators', researchers', and advocates' calls for establishing a more direct role for public schools in correcting historic imbalances and inequities—and attempts to provide a series of concrete actions to help schools move in that direction.

PART 1

DISTRICT POLICY AND
SCHOOL PRACTICE

CHAPTER ONE

■ ■ ■

An Overview of
High School Choice
in New York City

WITH NEARLY THREE MILLION foreign-born residents hailing from
well over a hundred different countries, New York City is one
of the most dynamic centers of immigration in the world.[1] New
York City's historic and enduring role in the United States' immigration narrative and its current leadership in urban school reform make it an unparalleled place in which to explore questions
about immigration, school choice, and educational equity in the
United States. Although the diversity and scope of immigration to
New York City is unmatched, cities and towns all over the country and the globe are now faced with the challenge of educating
immigrant-origin students, implementing reforms, and facilitating
immigrant families' integration into unfamiliar institutions like
schools.[2] Consequently, lessons learned in New York offer valuable examples for other education systems about how to respond
to new demands and ensure progress toward providing equitable
educational opportunities for all students through choice policies
and other mechanisms.

New York City is home to multiple, large immigrant communities. The "Hispanic" population alone is an extraordinarily heterogeneous, multiethnic group. According to the 2009 American Community Survey, the largest number of Hispanic immigrants in New York City hailed from the Dominican Republic (357,876), followed by Mexico (176,038), Ecuador (136,543), and Colombia (74, 904). Similar diversity is found among immigrants from Asia, Africa, Europe, and across the Caribbean.[3] City-wide data on the home languages, countries of origin, education and income levels of the foreign-born population provide a general sense of the diversity of New York's immigrant and immigrant-origin students as well. Experts estimate that as many 800 languages are spoken by New York City residents, and more than 125 countries of origin are represented.[4] Immigrants in New York, like in the rest of the United States, include some of the most educated and highly paid residents as well as some of the least educated and lowest income people.[5] In fact, data from the 2007 American Community Survey showed that 785,837 immigrants in New York State held college degrees, most of whom were living in the New York metropolitan area.[6]

New York City also has some of the greatest income inequality anywhere.[7] Poverty rates in New York City during the main years of the study ranged from 6 percent among non-Hispanic whites on Staten Island to a high of 36 percent among Hispanics in the Bronx (and an average of 18.7 percent overall). In fact, the gap between rich and poor was higher in Manhattan than in any other county in the entire United States.[8] These trends have only worsened since the economic downturn of 2008. Thus, the estimated 80,000 eighth-grade students who participate in high school choice each year in New York City come from families at the far extremes of the income and education continuum and include immigrants and children of immigrants with a wide variety of linguistic, cultural, and geographic origins.

The student population in New York City public schools mirrors the geographic and linguistic heterogeneity of the larger city-wide population. During the school year in which the majority of this research took place, just over one million students were enrolled in kindergarten through twelfth grade in New York City public schools. Hispanics comprised the largest racial/ethnic group (40.77 percent), followed by African American (35.33 percent), white (12.1 percent), and Asian/Pacific Islander students (10.68 percent).[9] The total number of foreign-born students and second-generation children of immigrants enrolled is not publicly released, so other figures must be used as a proxy for the size and characteristics of the immigrant-origin student population. The percentage of students classified as English language learners (ELL), "recent immigrants," and the results of the Home Language Identification Survey are three accessible data points. They indicate considerable geographic, linguistic, and socioeconomic heterogeneity among foreign-born and immigrant-origin students in New York City schools. An estimated 42 percent of students spoke a language other than English at home in the first year of the study, and in total, 176 different languages were documented.[10] Additionally, in 2009–2010, 14.4 percent of students were classified as English language learners, over two-thirds of whom spoke Spanish as their primary language. Finally, 2.1 percent of students in grades K–12 were considered "recent immigrants"—that is, foreign-born students who had arrived in New York City and enrolled in school in the United States for the first time in the past three years.

SCHOOL CHOICE IN NEW YORK CITY

School choice has been a longstanding focal point of education reform debates in New York City. Some version of high school choice has existed in New York City since the 1960s, and today parents in New York City may participate in choice at every stage of their child's public education, from prekindergarten through high school.[11] The Open Enrollment Program and Free Choice Transfer Policy began in New York City in 1963 and allowed students in high-minority schools to attend any school in the city with an open seat. These programs were directly linked to desegregation goals and are the forerunners to the current high school choice policy.[12]

Over time, the nature and purpose of school choice policies in New York City have changed. The goals and language have moved steadily away from explicit desegregation aims and toward infusing competition into the education marketplace. In recent years, district leaders have emphasized increasing the number of high-quality educational options for all students through the development of a "portfolio of schools."[13] The district's portfolio strategy is directly linked to expanding school choice with small school development and charter schools comprising two of its key elements. Amidst an array of choice options, the high school choice policy continues to be the New York City Department of Education's (NYCDOE) signature school choice initiative.

In theory, high school choice in New York City represents an opportunity to help interrupt enduring patterns of inequitable access to educational opportunities due to family income and racial/ethnic background. Through the choice process, low-income students from predominantly minority backgrounds who have historically attended the worst schools in the poorest neighborhoods can apply to attend any school across the city. Yet evidence to date has given little hope that school choice—in New York City and elsewhere—is successfully living up to its potential. Through an exploration of the ways in which high school choice actually plays out in diverse students' lives, *Unaccompanied Minors* begins to shed light on some of the limitations of many choice policies like New York City's and suggest actionable changes to policy and practice that may increase the likelihood of choice achieving its equity goals.

High School Application and Matching

Each year, an estimated 80,000 eighth-grade students choose from among 700 programs in approximately 400 public high schools across the city's five boroughs. To design the current iteration of the high school choice policy in New York City, the NYCDOE hired economists to develop a new algorithm to match students to high schools, and they modeled it after the National Resident Matching Program for American physicians.[14] The official goals for the revised policy were to increase both choice and equity for New York City public school families. To that end, the new high school "matching" formula was designed to improve the likelihood that a student would be assigned to his/her top choice and to distribute low-achieving students as evenly as possible across high schools.[15] Additionally, the number of schools/programs* that students could rank on their application was expanded from five to twelve.

The high school choice process officially begins in early fall when each eighth-grade student receives an individualized application form. The application is printed with a student's final seventh-grade report card grades in mathematics, English language arts, social studies, and science, his/her seventh-grade standardized test scores in reading and math, and average yearly attendance. These data determine a student's eligibility for certain "screened" schools and programs that have specific attendance, grade, and test score requirements. In addition, where applicable, a student's geographically zoned high school is listed at the top of the application. Not all students have a zoned high school, however, and twenty-one large high schools have been closed for poor performance since 2002, with additional high school closures announced each year amid considerable controversy.[16] A completed application is due by the first week of December.

High School Options and Admissions Criteria

New York City high schools run the gamut in terms of size, theme, specialization, and admissions criteria. Despite the push for small school creation, the majority of students continue to attend large, comprehensive high schools that serve more than 1,400 students.[17]

---

*Some schools host multiple programs that are organized around different curricular foci or specializations. On their applications, students list the individual programs within a school to which they are applying. Each program may have distinct admissions criteria.

Students may also attend career and technical high schools, small learning communities within high schools, and charter schools. (Charter schools do not participate in the choice process and instead admit students through a separate lottery system.)[18]

High schools in New York City use different selection criteria, and there are seven distinct mechanisms by which students gain entry into a particular school or program: "specialized" schools, screened schools, small schools, educational option, and zoned high schools. Each of these categories uses distinct admissions criteria. Among the most competitive high schools are the eight "specialized" schools that admit students based solely on their scores on an entrance examination, the Specialized High School Admissions Test (SHSAT); this test is offered annually to students in the fall of their eighth-grade year. Stuyvesant High School, perhaps the best known of the specialized high schools, first began restricting admission based on achievement in 1919, and in 1972 the New York State legislature passed the Hecht-Colandra Bill to formalize this practice and expand to three the number of schools that could use testing to determine admission.

The use of an entrance examination as the sole criterion for admission to the city's most elite schools has long come under fire on the grounds that the exam unfairly disadvantages low-income and minority students.[19] Such opposition continues today in the face of consistent underrepresentation of black and Latino students among those admitted to the specialized high schools. Black and Latino students comprised 70 percent of the city's public school student population in 2012–2013 and 53.6 percent of students who took the specialized high school admissions test that year. Yet they made up only 15 percent of students who received admission to any of the eight schools and only 12 percent for 2013–14.[20] Said differently, less than 6 percent of the approximately 12,500 black and Latino students who took the specialized test in fall 2012 were offered admission to any of the specialized high schools. In comparison, 35 percent of Asian and 30.6 percent of white students who took the SHSAT were offered seats. In light of this, the NAACP Legal Defense Fund, in conjunction with LatinoJustice Puerto Rican Legal Defense and Education Fund and the Center for Law and Social Justice at Medgar Evers College filed a federal civil rights complaint in September 2012 to challenge the specialized high school admissions process in New York City.

The specialized high schools serve only a fraction of the overall high school population, yet they often receive a disproportionate amount of public attention. There are many more seats available to students in the screened schools, small schools, educational option, and zoned high schools. Screened schools (or screened programs within a school) rank applicants based on their seventh-grade academic performance, standardized test scores, attendance, and punctuality; these schools and programs tend to be academically rigorous and highly sought-after. Educational option schools ("Ed-opt") choose students according to a bell curve whereby 16 percent of students accepted are in the high reading range on the city-wide seventh-grade standardized reading test, 68 percent are in the average reading range, and 16 percent are in the low reading range. The first such schools opened in the late 1960s and offered a way to integrate students of diverse academic levels.[21] A recent comprehensive analysis showed that the number of ed-opt schools has significantly decreased in recent years, thereby limiting the number of high performing school options for low-achieving students.[22]

By contrast, unscreened and limited unscreened schools have been serving an increasingly large share of New York City public school students over time. The majority of new small high schools fall into the category of limited unscreened; these schools do not have grade or test score requirements for admission but give priority to students who attend a school information session. Unscreened schools have no admissions requirements, and a computer randomly selects students based on available seats. Zoned schools are large comprehensive high schools that give priority to students who live in their geographic catchment area but do not have academic requirements for entry. Finally, some schools that concentrate on visual and performing arts require students to audition.

According to figures released by the New York City Department of Education, during the 2012–2013 school year roughly 84 percent of students were assigned to one of their top five choices.[23] In fact, NYCDOE reports that since the 2005–2006 high school admissions cycle, more than 80 percent of students have received one of their twelve choices in the first round each year. This also means, however, that approximately 10 percent of students, or about 8,000, are rejected by all of their choices and must participate in supplementary rounds in which fewer schools have spaces available.

NYCDOE has used the matching rates to tout the success of the high school choice policy, at least in terms of assigning students to their desired schools. Yet the validity of NYCDOE's reliance on the high school matching results to evaluate the policy's effectiveness has been called into question on the grounds that some students, particularly those with lower grades, are effectively barred from applying to some of the better schools in the city and have significantly fewer high-quality options.[24] In other words, even if students are assigned to schools that were on their application, many of them are ultimately relegated to attending schools with poor academic outcomes since those are the only schools for which they are eligible.[25]

Undersupply of High-Quality Educational Options

A basic problem in ensuring educational equity in New York City (and elsewhere) is the relative scarcity of high performing schools. After decades of perennial and widespread failure, New York City schools have shown some gains in recent years in terms of graduation rates and the percentage of students reaching proficiency on the National Assessment of Education Progress (NAEP).[26] However, the number of high performing high schools in the district remains severely limited. Graduation rates constitute only one measure of school quality, but they are a particularly important metric to consider given the significance of obtaining a high school diploma for lifetime earnings and other outcomes.[27] An analysis published by the Center for New York City Affairs at the New School found that only 38.3 percent of schools with graduating classes in 2007 had graduation rates of 75 percent or higher. This figure dropped to 12.6 percent when the more rigorous requirements for earning a Regents diploma were used.[28] Until 2012, New York State granted two categories of high school diplomas—local and Regents—based on the number of state-wide exit examinations ("Regents exams") passed. Starting with the entering ninth-grade class in the fall of 2008, the rules were changed so that all students must pass five Regents exams with a score of 65 or better in order to graduate; local diplomas are no longer awarded. By 2011, the results had changed only slightly. According to the author's own analysis of NYCDOE graduation rate data, the percentage of high schools with four-year graduation rates of 75 or above dropped to 34 percent (143 out of a total of 421 high schools), and only 20.2 percent of high schools (or a total of 85) had graduation rates of 75 percent or higher using the Regents diploma requirement. The dismal graduation outcomes provide strong evidence of the dearth of educational opportunities available to most students in New York City.

Schools in New York City also vary dramatically in terms of concentration of low-income students, safety records, teacher stability, student satisfaction, and college readiness rates, among other characteristics. The unevenness in school quality is shown in the publicly available *Progress Reports, Annual School Report Cards, Quality Reviews*, and *Learning Environment Surveys* published by NYCDOE. (See the appendix for a brief description of each of these documents and the high school choice materials made available by the department.)

The persistent undersupply of high performing high schools in the district foregrounds the need to examine the relationship between the design and implementation of the choice policy and the ultimate distribution of high-quality seats among a socioeconomically, racially, ethnically, linguistically, culturally, and academically diverse student population. Research to date on eighth-grade students' high school assignments by race/ethnicity in New York City shows that students of color are disproportionately enrolled in low performing schools.[29] Corcoran and Levin also found the high school choice policy to be ineffective in increasing racial/ethnic and income integration in New York City high schools.[30] Analyzing the high school applications and matching results for all eighth-grade students between 2005 and 2008, they found that on average, students were assigned to high schools that mirrored the socioeconomic and racial/ethnic makeup of their feeder middle schools despite having indicated preferences for schools that were less racially isolated and had smaller populations of free- and reduced-priced lunch eligible students than their middle schools.

Implications of Limited High-Quality Options

The current issues of supply and demand for high-quality schools exacerbate an already unbalanced distribution of educational opportunities in New York City. The substantial variation in graduation rates by high school and by students' racial/ethnic backgrounds points to some of the implications of the problem of undersupply. A four-year longitudinal report of the graduation rates for the class of 2011 showed that Hispanics had the lowest four-year graduation rates and highest dropout rates of any of the major racial/ethnic groups in the system. They were also the least likely to graduate with a Regents diploma. Black students also fared poorly relative to their white and Asian peers in terms of percent graduating after four years, percent dropping out, and rate of Regents diploma. By contrast, white and Asian students' graduation rates were above 75 percent in 2011, and almost all of them earned a Regents diploma.[31]

College readiness is one of the newest metrics being used by New York City and other districts to evaluate how schools are preparing students for postsecondary education. The results are similarly troubling. The New York State Department of Education developed a set of college readiness indicators in 2010 to assess the likelihood that a student would earn at least a C in a college-level course. They defined college readiness as scoring at least an 80 on the Math Regents exam and 75 on the English Regents. NYCDOE data showed that only 13 percent of black and Latino students currently graduate high school "college ready" compared to fifty percent of white and fifty percent of Asian students.[32] A more in-depth study of New York City students' college readiness found that the single strongest predictor of college readiness was neighborhood racial/ethnic composition.[33] There was a strong negative relationship between the percentage of black/Latino residents and college readiness scores. On the basis of these results, Fructer and his colleagues argued, "While high school choice may have improved educational options for individual students, choice has not been sufficient to increase system equity of opportunity . . . universal high school choice has not disrupted the relationship of demography to educational destiny across the city's struggling neighborhoods."[34]

CASE STUDY MIDDLE SCHOOL SITE

The arguments presented in this book are based on the results of a study conducted during two academic years (2008–2010) in New York City. The study combined ethnographic observations of school choice events, document analysis, parent and student interviews, and a case study of a middle school implementing the choice policy. The school "IS 725" served approximately 2,100 students in grades six through eight during the years of the study, and the student body was composed primarily of first-generation (foreign-born) and second-generation (U.S.-born) children of Latin American immigrants from the Dominican Republic, Mexico, Ecuador, and Colombia. Eighty percent of students were Hispanic, followed by 12 percent Asian (first- and second-generation students of Chinese, Indian, Bangladeshi, and Pakistani origin), 6 percent black, and 2 percent white. Over 80 percent of students qualified for free-or reduced-price lunch, and the school's high proportion of English language learners (37.9%) far outpaced the city-wide average of 14.1 percent in 2009–2010. With only 45.2 percent of students having scored at proficiency on the New York State mathematics exam in 2008–2009, IS 725 was considered a low performing school, and it was on the state's list of Schools in Needs of Improvement (SINI).

Upon enrollment in sixth grade, every student at IS 725 was assigned to one of five "academies," each with its own assistant principal, guidance counselor, and disciplinary dean. Students were also placed in an academic track: honors, regular, ESL, bilingual, special education, and gifted and talented, and they traveled to all major classes with the same group of students from their homeroom. Students in the gifted and talented track came from across the borough of Queens and were admitted based on the results of standardized exams; honors-track students had received recommendations from elementary school teachers or assigned based on elementary school performance. The juxtaposition of these two academically similar but socioeconomically and culturally distinct groups of students in one school allows for a more nuanced understanding of the institutional, individual, and family-level factors that contribute to *strategic* versus *passive* choice. Before delving into students' choice experiences, we must set the stage on which their choices were made by presenting the policy and school-level implementation efforts. We turn first to chapter 2, which provides a description of the high school choice policy according to district policy makers and an introduction to some of the faulty assumptions on which it was constructed.

—■■■—

CHAPTER TWO

An Imagined World
Flawed Assumptions About Schools, Students, and Families

The high school admissions process is centered on two principles: equity and choice. The student-driven process enables students to rank schools and programs in an order that accurately reflects their preferences . . . The Department of Education conducts workshops and fairs to help parents and students learn about the high school admissions process and make informed choice.

—New York City Department of Education[1]

IN ITS OFFICIAL description of high school choice, the New York City Department of Education (NYCDOE) presents the school choice process as a family endeavor in which students and parents, equipped with information provided by the district, are empowered to identify and apply to schools that most closely match students' interests and needs. NYCDOE has built a set of practices and procedures around these core tenets. Yet not all families follow NYCDOE's guidelines or behave in ways that conform to these expectations. What is more, the information that the district and

district theory vs family reality

school personnel develop and disseminate is often inadequate to prepare many families to select knowledgably from among seven hundred high school options city-wide.

The student-centered language in this official description also belies the district's actual perspective on how high school selection should unfold. Parents are assumed to be at the heart of eighth-grade students' high school choice experiences. In the eyes of NYCDOE, a student-driven process means one in which students will voice opinions and preferences about a set of high school options that has been predetermined by their parents. Parents are expected to take the reins in finding and organizing information, setting up school visits, and laying the groundwork for student-led decisions about which high schools to include on their applications. In other words, parents are tasked with narrowing the possibilities to those schools that they deem appropriate and that match their child's interests and needs. NYCDOE takes for granted that all parents will be engaged in these kinds of activities and, consequently, does not create a safety net for students who do not receive the anticipated forms of guidance and support at home. The chasm between district administrators' view of high school choice in theory and what many students and families actually experience in reality point to some of the limits to the district's realizing its stated equity goals through this choice policy.

DISTRICT OUTREACH AND COMMUNICATIONS EFFORTS

The New York City Department of Education narrowly defines its role and responsibilities in the high school choice process in terms of information provision. Consequently, it restricts its activities to explaining the steps of the process and furnishing public information about the vast number of available educational options. Each year, NYCDOE organizes roughly fifteen city-wide events including a city-wide high school fair, borough-based fairs, and a summer workshop series. It also publishes a variety of printed and electronic materials about the high school choice process. These include a six-hundred-page *Directory of New York City Public High Schools* distributed to each rising eighth-grade student and a number of short brochures and pamphlets that summarize different school types and offer tips to parents about how to work with their children to select high schools. Despite the volume of informational materials NYCDOE produces and the number of events they host, the impact and reach of the district's communication efforts are severely hindered by the format, content, and distribution methods used.

Information Asymmetry: Reliance on Electronic Media and Lack of Translated Materials

The weaknesses in NYCDOE's communication strategy vis-à-vis high school choice span from the production and content of materials to the modes of information dissemination. Specifically, NYCDOE's reliance on electronic resources and the lack of translated materials available in printed format means that people without Internet access and those who require materials in languages other than English are left with fewer official sources of information and guidance. For multiple school years, for example, the *High School Directory*, the most comprehensive resource on high schools in New York City, has only been made available in printed format in English. While the directory had been translated into the eight most commonly spoken languages (Spanish, Haitian-Creole, Russian, Chinese, Korean, Urdu, Bengali, and Arabic), the translated versions are only available electronically either on the NYCDOE website or through a compact disc distributed at choice events. Despite the exponential growth in Internet access and usage in the twenty-first century, research shows that computer literacy and Internet access continues to be strongly correlated with income and education level.[2] As a result, getting even basic information about schools may be considerably more difficult for people on the disadvantaged side of the "digital divide."

The question of families' Internet access notwithstanding, there are substantial costs associated with downloading and printing a six-hundred-page document. Yet other than the single-page description of each high school in the directory, virtually no information about individual schools was readily accessible in printed format during the years of this study. The same was true of the *Learning Environment Surveys, Quality Reviews, Progress Reports,* and *Annual School Report Cards*—school-level reports containing more detailed information about performance and academic outcomes such as graduation rates, credit accumulation, and student proficiency on state examinations.

NYCDOE also depends heavily on third-party websites to assist families with school choice. In a number of official publications, students and parents are referred to Internet-based resources such as HopStop.com or the Metropolitan Transit Authority website to get estimated travel times to different schools. NYCDOE's repeated instructions to use the directory to identify schools and to conduct additional research on the Internet does not take into account that some families do not have printed versions of the directory in their home language or the means or skills to use the Internet as a research tool. Knowing and understanding the "rules of the game" of high school choice in New York City was a critical element of the more informed participants' eventual success in securing desired high school placements; the series of linguistic and technological obstacles in place made it more difficult for certain families—namely, lower income and non-English dominant students and parents—to learn these rules in order to play the game and, ultimately, to gain access to high-quality educational opportunities through choice.

Minimal School Performance Data Provided

Beyond NYCDOE's reliance on Internet-based sources of information and its failure to print translated publications, there were considerable shortcomings in the actual information provided and in the messages NYCDOE transmitted in print and in person. The exclusion of school performance from the list of important decision-making factors in school selection was one of the most striking lacunae in NYCDOE communications.

Discussion of how to assess school performance and why this might be a worthwhile school selection criterion was missing entirely from school choice publications. Moreover, it was mentioned only once in the eight live presentations observed. Instead, students' academic and extracurricular interests, school location, and school size were repeatedly highlighted as vital characteristics to consider when choosing schools. Furthermore, aside from a brief paragraph hidden in the directory, families received no explicit instruction about the type of school performance information that was publicly available or how to access it. This was particularly surprising in light of the multimillion dollar investment that NYCDOE had made in 2007 and 2008 to create the *Learning Environment Survey Reports, Quality Review Reports*, and *Progress Reports*, which contain a variety of school outcomes data.

The *Directory of the New York City Public High Schools* is a telephone-book-sized publication composed of individualized descriptions of New York City's approximately four hundred high schools. The directory that was in use at the time of my study included the school's address, contact information, programs offered, and eligibility requirements for each program. The first pages of the directory provided general information about the high school choice process and reviewed the different school types and selection methods (e.g., specialized high schools, screened, edopt). A single page in the directory presented a list of the different school-level reports that were publicly available and a link to the website where they could be accessed; however, this list was buried between a paragraph about the services available for students with special needs and a list of schools deemed "in need of improvement" (SINI) by the State of New York.

Significantly, the one-page description of the school-level reports was the only place in the entire directory in which some of the traditional school-quality metrics—graduation rates, Regents passing rates, and credit accumulation—were mentioned by name. These important data points were not provided on the individual school pages, however, and the onus of finding this information was thus placed on students and parents. Furthermore, while the descriptions of these indicators found in the directory were quite limited and did not explicitly use the language of "quality," it was the only publication that made reference to using these data as a tool to evaluate and compare school performance.[3] Discussion of what constitutes a high-quality or high performing high school and how to find this information was similarly omitted from live presentations made by NYCDOE staff and from the PowerPoint presentation that NYCDOE provided to middle school guidance counselors to use at their schools.

NYCDOE confined its involvement in high school choice to the single task of providing information to students and families about how the choice process works and the educational options available across the city. However, evidence from students and parents participating in the choice process shows that the district's efforts fell considerably short of meeting its constituents' needs. Flaws in NYCDOE's overall strategy to help families participate in a mandatory high school choice process extend far beyond its inadequate approach to communications. District administrators espoused faulty assumptions about student engagement and held unrealistic expectations of parental involvement. There was also a complete lack of infrastructure set up at the school level to provide much-needed guidance and support, and district leadership failed to articulate clear, enforceable expectations of school personnel's involvement in the choice process. Each of these issues weakened the equity potential of the choice policy in its own right, but combined, the detrimental impacts were multiplied.

UNREALISTIC EXPECTATIONS OF PARENTAL INVOLVEMENT IN CHOICE

NYCDOE administrators' imagined version of high school choice revolved around the assumption that parents would spearhead the entire process. This idea was based in large part on NYCDOE administrators' presumption of parents' familiarity with their children's academic strengths and weaknesses. Time and time again,

NYCDOE representatives communicated their belief that parents would know their child's academic skills in great depth and detail and would use this information to determine the most suitable high school selections. Yet data from parents and students in this study as well as other research on class- and culturally based differences in parental involvement in education challenge this idea.[4]

District and borough-based staff repeatedly made comments to the effect that parents would or should be intimately familiar with their child's academic abilities, interests, and needs. At one high school choice informational event held for sixth- and seventh-grade parents in the Bronx, a representative from the borough enrollment office began her presentation by stating, "Parents, you know better than anybody what your child is capable of and what his strengths are." She then proceeded to name the myriad tasks they were charged with in the choice process, such as reviewing the *High School Directory*, researching schools on the Internet, attending information sessions and open houses, meeting with guidance counselors, and checking the completed application to approve the high schools that their child had listed.

A NYCDOE administrator echoed this perspective at the citywide high school fair, held annually during one fall weekend at a large high school in Brooklyn. Addressing an auditorium teeming with nearly six hundred parents, students, and family members, he declared, "Nobody knows your child better than you—their strengths, academic weaknesses, interests." He then launched into a litany of instructions about what parents should be doing to prepare for high school choice. Notably, references to the role of middle school personnel or even to eighth-grade students themselves were conspicuously missing from his description of the school search process.

NYCDOE officials' recurring remarks provide one example of the pervasive expectations of parents as agenda-setters in the choice process. The exhaustive list of recommended activities for parents and students to engage in before completing the high school application is another. These activities, which were cited recurrently at workshops and in publications, reflect NYCDOE's understanding of the proper division of labor between the district and families—where the district's role is narrowly defined in terms of information provision, and within families—where parents were supposed to lead the information-gathering and school identification and students were to give input on final school selections. The size and scope of the list of suggested steps also bring to light the complexity of the process that students and parents were asked to negotiate.

How to Navigate the Citywide High School Fair is one of the most widely distributed documents produced by NYCDOE. It provides a window into the district's perspective on what families should be doing to winnow the seven hundred possibilities to no more than the application's limit of twelve schools/programs and, ultimately, to successfully participate in the high school choice process. Furthermore, it explicitly names the volume of tasks that were recommended to students and parents.

The two-and-a half-page document begins by enumerating a series of activities that should be completed in advance of families' attendance at the city-wide high school fair. Under the heading "Come Prepared," bulleted suggestions include: "Have several conversations with your child about his/her interests, transportation considerations, etc.," "Use small Post-it notes to mark those pages [in the High School Directory] of the schools you want to visit at the fair," "Write down questions that you might have on the school's page or the Post-it note," and "Once you have identified the schools in which you and your child are interested, conduct additional research" by going to the school's website and looking at the Learning Environment Survey Report, Quality Review Report, Progress Report, and Annual School Report Card. Beyond listing these reports as one way to learn more about a school, however, the document does not provide any explanation of the information they contain or how the reports might be useful. Furthermore, no instructions are given about how to retrieve these reports if people do not have Internet access.

NYCDOE also generated a series of twenty questions for parents to ask school representatives at the high school fairs. Topics ranged from school culture, the freshman program, acceleration, remediation, and intervention services to average class size, uniforms, and dates of open houses and tours. After the fair, parents are instructed to "Fold the corner of the pages of the schools you visited," "Review the schools with your child," "Decide if you would like to go to the open house to learn more about a particular school," and, "If you visited the exhibit of any schools that you did not research previously, take time to research them . . . in preparation for the Borough Fairs." This final set of tasks is supposed to be completed within forty-eight hours of attendance at the city-wide fair. Taken together, these suggestions reveal NYCDOE's lofty expectations of what families should do to "make the right choice." Furthermore, the document provides a sketch of an ideal model of what the search for high schools should look like according to the people who designed the policy.

This brochure reflects NYCDOE administrators' belief in the importance of attending the city-wide high school fair for effective participation in high school choice. Yet less than half of eighth-graders who must submit applications each year attend the fair, according to attendance figures.[5] NYCDOE publishes additional materials that include suggested activities beyond attending the city-wide fair; however, its heavy emphasis on one event that over half of the school choice participants do not attend is representative of the leadership's overall disconnect with the ways in which many of its constituents are actually engaging in, preparing for, and understanding choice.

GUIDANCE COUNSELORS IN NYCDOE'S IMAGINED VERSION OF CHOICE

In NYCDOE administrators' breakdown of school choice duties, school personnel (namely, guidance counselors) were understood to be the district's front-line representatives for interfacing with students and parents about high school choice. In fact, district officials described in detail what they thought middle school guidance counselors should be doing to inform, assist, and guide students and families through the complex web of high school choice. However, the district did not establish minimum standards for what each middle school must do to prepare its students and parents to choose high schools, nor did it monitor or evaluate school personnel's actions. Instead, schools were left to determine what resources and personnel, if any, would be allocated to working with families on high school choice. Data from the case-study middle school presented in chapter 4 show how radically school-level approaches could depart from NYCDOE administrators' ideal in the absence of proper guidelines, incentives, and supervision.

In its various school choice materials, NYCDOE identifies the middle school guidance counselor as the primary point person to whom all high school choice questions should be directed. District administrators also stated this explicitly at the different workshops held across the city. For instance, at one Manhattan event, a central office staff person urged the audience of over two hundred adults and children:

> Please, please you can never underestimate the guidance counselor in your school. They are really an extension of us. There is no way we can meet your guidance needs at the central office . . . Work in tandem with the counselors as much as you can. You can get their buy-in as to which programs make the most sense to put on the application.

At the city-wide fair, the importance of guidance counselors was mentioned at least four times over the course of an hour-long presentation. At one point, the NYCDOE administrator said:

> It is very, very important that you work closely with your child's guidance counselor . . . That's their job—not just for the specialized high schools. You should have an open line of communication with your child's guidance counselor—not only phone calls and visiting

but also email. So you should get the guidance counselor's email and communicate with he or she [*sic*] that way.

Parents were also advised to meet with their child's guidance counselor before handing in the application to "Make sure they know about your choices, whether or not they make the most sense and you are making the most use of your twelve choices." Finally, while one borough enrollment director told the audience at a workshop that "The guidance counselors aren't always as informed about the schools. It is really up to parents," she also suggested that parents consult with the guidance counselor by "Ask[ing] what they know about your child that you might not know. This might help you understand your child better and choose appropriate schools." Despite frequent references to the ways in which guidance counselors could assist families with the high school application, NYCDOE neither developed formal requirements nor established a baseline number of activities that schools or guidance counselors had to complete in preparation for students' submission of the high school application. What is more, every time guidance counselors were mentioned, either in publications or at workshops, it was ultimately left to parents to initiate contact, make requests for assistance, and ask questions.

Limited Oversight of School-Level Activities

NYCDOE staff members had limited contact with school personnel in matters related to the high school choice process. While they offered optional training for guidance counselors about how the choice process works and how to use the online system to enter students' applications, there was no compulsory professional development. As a result, district staff only interacted with those school personnel who sought them out, and they knew very little about what happened on the ground. When central office employees did have an opportunity to engage with middle school guidance counselors, the discussions usually centered on administrative tasks related to the application. For example, when asked during an interview about the content of the training, district administrators responsible for the choice process only mentioned discussions that took place regarding the technical aspects of the application process; conversely, topics such as the appropriate role for guidance counselors and expectations of the type of assistance they would provide to students and families were not referenced. One administrator described the training in the following way: "Well, we mostly talk about the [application entry] system itself, the mechanics of navigating the system, how they have to enter things into the computer."

NYCDOE staff also used the training sessions to remind guidance counselors of the deadline for entering all the eighth-grade students' applications in the online system. As one district official explained: "We make sure that the counselors know the deadlines, that they are able to do this in a timely fashion. We want them to get all of the applications in on time so we don't have to keep asking. It's a tough part of the process." In fact, one of the few ways in which the central staff could actually monitor middle school guidance counselors was by tracking when they entered student applications. Another way was by counting the number of appeals their students made after they received their high school assignments in early spring. District representatives reported that this was one way they could assess how successful guidance counselors were at informing families about the choice process:

> We can look at the data, monitor when the applications are being entered. We can see if this work is getting done. And we want it on time. For us, it is really important that the work gets done and done on time. A lot of times, it's kind of hard because we do have to follow up with individual guidance counselors or schools. The eighth-grade counselor procrastinates and waits until right before the deadline. The system can't handle the volume . . . If we don't see activity we contact them—sometimes the guidance counselor directly or, if we need to bump it up, sometimes we contact the principal. And the

principal might not have any idea about the deadline or when it gets done. They have so much going on.

In contrast to their access to school-level data about when the applications were entered, NYCDOE administrators had no way of knowing what guidance counselors actually did to explain the choice process to students and families. This lack of oversight existed despite the fact that the district representatives expressed clear ideas about what they thought the guidance counselors should be doing. When asked to describe guidance counselors' responsibilities in the choice process, the interview respondents first named a series of administrative duties: distributing directories, handing out individual applications, and collecting and entering applications before the deadline. They also cited a range of additional activities in which they expected guidance counselors to engage to support families during the application process:

> Explain the mechanics of the process. Follow up with families. Do guidance presentations to the classes, to the eighth-grade classes, for example. Work closely with the families. Be proactive in monitoring the applications; look at distance from home—making sure it isn't too far. Making sure the student is eligible for the program or that it is a good fit based on what the guidance counselor knows about the student.

This description placed substantially more burden on school personnel to insert themselves as advisors into the process than what was found in publications or in the commentaries made during public events. Yet despite a concrete vision for what good school-based support for eighth-grade families looked like, NYCDOE officials had neither leverage nor tools at their disposal to mandate such actions. As one of the interviewees explained, "Well, we can't really see what each guidance counselor is doing. It has to happen at the school level. The AP [assistant principal] or principal, if that's part of the rubric that they use to evaluate the guidance counselor then maybe it can show up there."

The district administrators were also well aware of the extreme variability in the quality of guidance counselors and in the extent of the support provided to families. One described the range in guidance counselors' engagement as follows:

> Guidance counselors, when they enter the choices into the system, are not really paying attention to them. So, this tells them. Of course, there are always some counselors who feel like, "I don't care as long as they get it [the application] in." You have a bell curve: there are always some good ones and some not so good.

In addition, NYCDOE officials made note of the fact that the high school choice process might be of little import to middle school principals who had no reason other than altruistic ones for dedicating school resources to helping students get into top schools. These comments get at the heart of one of the main equity issues in the overall design and implementation of the choice policy: the lack of school-level accountability for preparing students and parents to participate in the choice process.

> I think that as a principal, you would like to see your middle school students getting into the specialized schools, the ritzy programs. If you get a lot of kids into those kinds of schools, it is kind of like a feather in your cap. It might help you recruit elementary school kids to your school also. Not everyone thinks along those lines though or even thinks it is relevant at all. It's really up to the principal. They all want their kids to do well, to graduate . . .

> I'm not convinced that they [principals] are incentivized at all. They are not given any incentives to be more engaged in the process. Of course, they care about their students—they want them to be promoted, to graduate. But beyond that I don't think there is necessarily a focus on getting kids into their top choices or into the screened programs. They look at a set of kids and they want them to do well.

NYCDOE administrators were well aware that middle school principals and guidance counselors lacked external motivation or incentives to provide the extensive support and guidance that they envisioned. However, they did not suggest central office involvement to help solve this problem, either through increased oversight or top-down initiatives to increase school-level assistance to families. Instead, the respondents singularly described the role of the central office in terms of leading a city-wide effort to disseminate information and providing on-demand support to borough and school-based staff when necessary.

Tellingly, NYCDOE officials referred to the problem of information asymmetry among eighth-grade students and families on a number of occasions without prompting. However, they did not point to differences in middle schools' engagement with families as the root of the issue. Instead, they articulated a need to diversify city-wide outreach strategies and simplify information:

> As much as we trumpet this as a choice process, not everyone has equal information . . . This is the danger—an unlevel playing field. Some families are more equipped to navigate it. We try to conduct outreach to every part of the city. We do workshops, fairs . . . We try to reach out as broadly as possible. We try to find as many different ways to hit as many of the families we can. There is an opportunity to improve—we still have a long way to go . . . I don't think we're there. We tend to rely a lot on the same ways of doing things. We need to do different things to reach people we aren't getting to . . . Because we are really just reaching the same people.

Thus, while district officials recognized the ongoing inadequacies of their outreach and communication practices, they restricted their analysis of the problem to a city-wide perspective. Consequently, the only proffered changes were to those parts of the process for which they were directly responsible, that is, providing information to families at a city-wide level through publications, workshops, and fairs. At the same time, they virtually ignored the possibility of the central headquarters playing a role in improving school-level approaches to working with families—for example, by developing enforceable guidelines and requirements for what schools must do to prepare students and parents to participate in high school choice or by mandating training for relevant school personnel. Ultimately, district representatives failed to recognize the need for greater institutional involvement in families' choice experiences for policies such as high school choice in New York City to promote greater educational equity.

PARENTS' INFORMATION NEEDS AND DESIRES

The voices of three parents provide a window into the mismatch between NYCDOE's communications and outreach efforts and the information, support, and guidance that some families want and need from schools and from NYCDOE. These parents express desire for help and dissatisfaction with the lack of formal opportunities to receive detailed, personalized information and advice about choosing high schools in New York City. Maria, a U.S.-born woman of Puerto Rican descent in her early forties, had already been through the high school choice process with two older children when it was time for her third son, Danny, to pick high schools. Yet she still found it difficult to access information and help him make decisions about schools. Maria critiqued the choice process on a number of fronts:

> It should start earlier. There should be more information given to parents—websites that you could look at for dates and stuff. The book [*High School Directory*] had some information but it was hard to know when they had visits, open houses. Sometimes you can't even make an appointment for the visit. Or if you can't make it on the date, that's it. A lot of times you can call the number listed and nobody answers.

Lanisha, a first-time participant in New York City's high school choice process, called for a more concrete role for her daughter's guidance counselors than what NYCDOE representatives had suggested. She also pointed to one of the myriad aspects of the process that families found difficult and confusing—understanding how to determine the schools for which a child is a competitive applicant.

> I think the guidance counselor should have sat down with all of the students and talked to them about their future, what they wanted to do, and give them a list of schools to choose from in the neighborhood or that fit based on that . . . They should have each child sit with the guidance counselor and do an assessment to find out what they want to do, what they are good at. Then, based on the assessment, give them the schools that are available to them. Like give the child a checklist of things to check and from that you can know which schools are good . . . Instead it was hard to know which schools were right and which ones she had a chance to get accepted at.

Antonio, the Dominican-born stepfather of a recent immigrant student who is profiled at length later in the book, echoed Lanisha's demand for clear instructions and an indication of which schools were "good." For his part, Antonio called on the NYCDOE to publish a list of recommended schools to help families avoid the worst options:

> Now, my opinion is that the secretary of education, or the board of education as it is called, they should, because they have all of the complaints, right? From all of the schools. Then who would be better to know which ones are good and which are bad? So they should send a separate list that says, "This school has this record, this school has this, this school this." Every school with its record, you see? So that one could know which to avoid. Because without this parents only go to the ones that they've heard about, if they've heard anything. [translated from Spanish by the author]

In their own words, these parents explicitly identify the type of detailed information they wanted and the nature of guidance they felt was needed to smoothly negotiate the application process. Yet, as chapter 3 shows, they and the majority of parent respondents from IS 725 did not receive nor have easy access to the desired information. Moreover, they had minimal contact with their child's school regarding the high school application. These interviews begin to tell the story of the extent to which NYCDOE and the guidance counselors at IS 725 missed the mark in terms of preparing, informing, and supporting students and families with their high school choice-making—a central theme explored throughout this book.

A POLICY BUILT ON SHAKY GROUND

NYCDOE relies on a broad set of assumptions about parents' knowledge of their children in the design and implementation of its policy of high school choice. It also maintains an expectation of high levels of parental involvement in choosing high schools. NYCDOE's anticipation of significant parental engagement reflects an underlying belief in the forces of the educational marketplace to stimulate parental action.

Some of the earliest proponents of the idea of school choice predicted that it would spawn greater parental participation in their children's schooling.[6] Political scientists John Chubb and Terry Moe argued, "In a system where virtually all the important choices are the responsibilities of others, parents have little incentive to be informed or involved. In a market-based system much of the responsibility would be shifted to parents (their choices would have consequences for their children's education), and their incentives to become informed and involved would be dramatically different."[7] While their assertion that school choice would transfer additional responsibilities to parents proved accurate in the case of the high school choice process in New York City, the theory that choice would automatically produce greater incentives for parental involvement and increased information-seeking was erroneous.

Subsequent chapters show that some students and parents—typically, of higher socioeconomic backgrounds—were keenly aware of and likely to engage in NYCDOE-sanctioned search strategies. They read NYCDOE publications and attended informational events; received advice from friends, relatives, and members of their social network who were familiar with high school choice; or they had previous relevant experiences such as participating in middle school choice in New York City. Many of them also shared NYCDOE's understanding of the proper role of parents in children's education or, if they were children, lived in homes where this was the prevailing view. By virtue of being more attuned to NYCDOE's messages about choice, these students and parents were more easily able to develop and use an *institutional compass*—the ability to negotiate complex institutions and processes—to navigate the choice system. (For more about strategic choice and the idea of an institutional compass, see chapter 4.)

By contrast, students and parents who consumed fewer NYCDOE school choice materials, were less familiar with the strengths and weaknesses of the school system overall, and whose family dynamics, norms, and child-rearing practices were distinct from those assumed or anticipated by district administrators (generally, lower income and immigrant-origin) engaged in choice far differently from NYCDOE's proposed model. They operated within a distinct context and under a set of constraints that NYCDOE failed to take into account in its design and implementation of the policy; consequently, few were able to develop or use an institutional compass to their advantage in choosing high schools.

NYCDOE's approach to high school choice represents an all-too-common pattern: school systems continually fail to create the necessary conditions for equity-driven policies to live up to their promise to facilitate better educational opportunities for historically disadvantaged students. Inadequate communication methods and faulty assumptions of students and parents only tell part of the story of NYCDOE's misguided efforts to put in place an equity-minded school choice policy. In the chapter that follows, we look at school-level implementation of high school choice and, specifically, guidance counselors' behaviors and perspectives. We see firsthand how the absence of formal requirements for school-based activities around school choice exacerbate difficulties for parents and students in an educational environment dominated by regulation and accountability.

■ ■ ■

CHAPTER THREE

Unenforced Expectations
Tensions Between
Accountability and Choice

THE LIGHTS ARE dimmed and the air-conditioner is on full blast as roughly one hundred eighth-grade students from Academy B shuffle into the first-floor auditorium at IS 725. It is a warm fall day in late September, and the bell for second period has already rung. The assistant principal for Academy B, Danielle DiSpirito, an Italian American woman in her late thirties, stands at the front of the auditorium loudly instructing students to sit down in the first few rows. Ms. Perolli, the academy's guidance counselor—a petite, white woman who speaks in a thick New York accent—stands next to Ms. DiSpirito arranging plastic transparencies on an overhead projector. After about three minutes all students have taken their seats, removed their headphones, spit out their gum, and quieted down.

Ms. DiSpirito opens the assembly by explaining the purpose:

> Ms. Perolli is going to talk to you today about the high school selec-
> tion process. Many of you have been going to her, asking the same

questions, so she decided to take time out of her day to do this presentation. Listen to her with your ears and brain open because I know that you are going to have a zillion questions for her that she probably has answered today. If you have individual questions for her after this, then you can go talk to her.

For the remaining thirty-five minutes of the period, Ms. Perolli uses grainy overhead transparencies to review the mechanics of the application process, describe the information found in the *High School Directory*, suggest characteristics to consider when selecting schools, and offer tips for improving students' chances of getting accepted to competitive schools. Referring to a photocopied image of a sample page from the directory, Ms. Perolli begins by advising students to first check school location:

> All right, guys, I hope that you've been looking through the *High School Directory* that I handed out in June . . . This is a sample page . . . Where you need to focus is on the box with the address so you can get the information you need. You might be thinking, "Big deal, Ms. P." Well, it is a big deal . . . Location is very, very important. You have to be there early in the morning, stay late for afterschool activities, travel there when the weather is bad. So you have to make sure you are willing to travel there. You can go visit and test out how far it is. Go to the school on Saturday with your parents would be my suggestion. What trains, what buses do you need to get there? It's very, very important where a school is located.

Ms. Perolli then proceeds to describe the various selection methods (screened, specialized exam, audition, ed-opt, limited unscreened, and zoned). She presents a sample application and tells students that, unlike in years past when students automatically had a seat reserved in their zoned school, they must now list their zoned school on the application to be guaranteed a spot. She also suggests that if students want a particular screened program but are not academically eligible for it, they should apply to every other program in that school and try to switch once they get there: "You're gonna get in the door. The point is you are going to get into a program and then you can switch, but you are in that school."

The presentation ends with a reminder about the required parental signature at the bottom of the application: "I cannot accept an application without a parent or guardian's signature. I would hope that you are going over this with your parents, discussing it with them." When she solicits questions from the audience only one student raises his hand. His voice is drowned out by the chatter of students, and Ms. Perolli tells him to come to her office later.

Before dismissing the students, Ms. DiSpirito makes a closing announcement:

> When it comes to the applications, they not only need to be signed by your parents, but you also need to turn it in on time. Ms. P needs to sit in her office and enter each one of them by hand; there is no computer to do it automatically. So if you make a mistake, she'll give it back to you. I am not expecting her to correct the mistakes of 150 students. That's not her job. Every year we get the same thing: "I don't like this school, I don't want to go there, it's too far." Be prepared to get into any school on your list or to not get accepted to any school. No matter how many times your parents call to complain, we cannot switch your school. The best we can do is tell you how you can fill out the application . . . And I warned you about your grades in seventh grade. Now that you are in eighth grade you really need to pass all of your classes. There was one girl who got an acceptance letter from a high school but didn't pass her classes . . . It starts now.

Students in Academy B received an abbreviated version of these instructions from Ms. Perolli a few weeks later when she visited each homeroom to distribute their individualized application forms. At least half of them (roughly sixty-five students) also met with her in small groups over the course of the next two months when she found time to call them down to her office to discuss their applications. However, Ms. Perolli was unable to meet individually with every eighth-grade student from her academy, and for a number of them, the large, impersonal auditorium presentation constituted the only form of school-based information they received about the application process.

THE CONSEQUENCES OF UNENFORCED EXPECTATIONS

This first vignette shows how far removed school-based outreach efforts can be from the personalized support and direct communication with families that New York City Department of Education administrators described and anticipated in the previous chapter. NYCDOE officials widely expressed their view—in printed materials, at city-wide informational events, and in personal interviews—of middle school counselors as central figures in facilitating students' high school choices. Yet the district neither developed formal requirements nor established a baseline number of activities that schools or guidance counselors had to complete to assist students with high school choice. Moreover, school-level actions were not monitored or factored into any school evaluations. Instead, schools were left to determine what resources and personnel, if any, would be allocated to working with families on the application process.

Without guidelines, mandates, incentives, or supervision, evidence from IS 725 shows that school-level approaches could depart radically from the district officials' ideas of what should happen. With caseloads of approximately four hundred students across grades six through eight, on any given day a guidance counselor at IS 725 might be leading a mandated counseling session, participating in a disciplinary meeting, conducting an exit interview for a student who had been discharged, and/or processing a new student enrollment. The tasks related to the high school choice process were piled on top of these daily responsibilities. Taking cues from the school leadership, the guidance counselors at IS 725 viewed high school choice as little more than a required administrative burden to be completed as quickly and efficiently as possible.

High School Choice as a Low-Priority Policy

In spite of the well-established significance of the transition to high school for adolescent development and achievement and NYCDOE's public pronouncements of the centrality of choice in its strategic reform efforts, the high school choice process proved to be an issue of minimal consequence to the school administration and guidance counselors at IS 725.[1] In the absence of oversight, mandates, incentives, or sanctions, NYCDOE's expectations of extensive school-level guidance in choosing high schools were unrealized at IS 725. Instead, students and families received minimal assistance with their high school applications and were left alone to negotiate the complex system.

The school's failure to host even a single informational event for parents about the high school choice process is perhaps the strongest indication of the extent to which school-level implementation of the choice policy deviated from district officials' view of what should take place. Notably, during the school year prior to the in-depth year of study, guidance counselors at IS 725 worked in conjunction with the community outreach coordinator on staff to organize an evening program for 250 students and parents about the high school choice process. Ms. Perolli led the event, and, using a PowerPoint presentation furnished by NYCDOE, she reviewed the steps of the process, explained how to use the extensive *High School Directory* to identify suitable schools, and provided additional suggestions and commentary while Mr. Sanchez, a bilingual guidance counselor, translated simultaneously in Spanish. After the meeting, attendees were invited to visit the cafeteria where different Queens high schools had set up information booths staffed by high school students and school representatives ready to answer questions.

The following year IS 725 did not host any school-wide event for families of eighth-grade students. Guidance counselors offered varied explanations why, and their responses reveal the lack of principal oversight of school-based activities to inform eighth-grade students and parents about high school choice. Their accounts also indicate the lack of initiative and/or support from the administration (and the district) to dedicate time, resources, and personnel to work with families on choice in ways that were consistent with what NYCDOE officials envisioned, even when guidance counselors were interested in doing so.

As early as the second week of September, Ms. Perolli described her ideas for the type of parent information session that she would like the school to organize that year: "I know that this year money is tight, but I want to tell him [the principal] that we should have two Saturdays in October when school is open and we, guidance counselors, are available to answer questions for students and parents. I would be here for students who have questions. We could put the word out." Mr. Sanchez echoed her interest in a Saturday event, explaining: "I prefer doing it on Saturday because I can come in with much more energy." However, by mid-November of that year, with less than three weeks remaining before the deadline for students to submit their applications, no event, workshop, or open house had been planned. Mr. Sanchez explained the lack of event as a function of the budget: "The principal has a lot going on. It's a lot of pressure. He left it up to the guidance counselors this year, but I couldn't do it all on my own. It just never happened. I'm not sure why. People just didn't get it together. And I couldn't do it all on my own." For her part, Ms. Perolli attributed it to the fact that Ms. Torres, the community coordinator whom she believed to be responsible for planning such an event, was pregnant and did not do it. In the end, no steps were taken to address the confusion, and no one took the reins in planning.

The principal of a low-performing middle school of 2,100 students faces substantial pressure to improve student achievement in the post–No Child Left Behind era. It is therefore not entirely unexpected that Principal Robert Polo was either unaware or unconcerned that a parent workshop about high school choice had not been organized. It was more surprising, however, that the assistant principals in charge of each academy (of approximately four hundred students) did not notice or did not seem to be bothered by the fact that no high school choice event had taken place. Conversations with assistant principals (APs) confirmed their lack of concern and limited involvement in tasks related to high school choice. The APs' responses also showed the true division of labor at IS 725—one in which guidance counselors were left wholly responsible for the range of activities associated with high school choice.

Ms. Cipriano, the AP in charge of Academy C, explicitly stated her lack of involvement in the high school choice process. She responded to a request for an interview about her role in high school choice by stating, "I'm not that involved in the process . . . I help if the guidance counselor asks me to intervene, but it's really up to the guidance counselor who is in charge of it." Ms. Cutler, from Academy A, made remarks to a similar effect and admitted that she had "no idea" what the guidance counselor in her academy had done to explain the high school application to students. Hence, all levels of the school administration at IS 725 treated the high school choice process as an issue of minor significance, and it was left to guidance counselors alone to determine how to implement the policy without any resources at their disposal.

Under these conditions, the guidance counselors at IS 725 treated high school choice as a necessary chore, and they attempted to minimize its demands on their time. They did so even while knowing that many of their eighth-grade students were unprepared to make informed school selections. In fact, guidance counselors actually expected that many students and parents would be confused by the choice process and anticipated that they would be unhappy with their final high school assignments. However, rather than increase outreach efforts or change their approaches to working with students on high school choice, the counselors relied on the same communication strategies year after year to explain the process—even when they had clear ideas for how this could be improved.

Guidance Counselors' Approaches to Informing Students About High School Choice

Guidance counselors struggled to complete an exhaustive list of technical requirements associated with the high school choice process, and they received limited support from their colleagues to do so. In June and September they distributed copies of the *High School Directory* to all rising eighth-grade students; in October, they handed out personalized high school applications to every eighth-grader; they returned to classrooms to exhort students to bring in completed applications by the first week of December; they reviewed each submitted application to confirm that it had been signed by a parent/guardian; they entered each student's application manually into the online computer system, listing every unique program code (up to twelve); they consulted with students who had listed invalid program codes or programs for which they were ineligible in order to replace it with a valid option; they made changes to applications that had already been entered when parents made formal written requests to do so; and finally, they followed up individually with students who had not brought in their applications by the deadline by calling them to their offices, calling their homes, and requesting that parents deliver the application in person. These tasks constituted only one part of the year-long high school choice process. Students who do not get matched to any high school in the first round must participate in a supplementary round in March. During the 2008–2009 school year, for example, approximately 7,500 students city-wide, or 9 percent of the total population of eighth-graders who submitted high school applications, did not receive a school assignment. In addition, each year a number of students appeal their assignments; in 2007–2008, 3,722 students made requests for an appeal.[2] At IS 725, over 100 students were deferred to the supplementary round, and nearly the same number requested appeals the year in which the study took place. Thus, for guidance counselors, the high school choice process persists for the entire duration of the school year.

In an effort to reduce the amount of time that high school choice demanded of them, the guidance counselors at IS 725 concentrated their energies on two main goals: collecting a completed application from every eighth-grade student by the deadline and limiting the number of future appeals requests. Their focus on meeting a deadline rather than on facilitating appropriate student choices resulted in their providing superficial, operational information to students, interacting only rarely with parents, and offering negligible personalized advice to the hundreds of low-income and immigrant-origin eighth-grade students at the school—students who would likely have benefited from additional assistance in making high school choices. As limited as Ms. Perolli's outreach strategy was, in fact, it was the most extensive and informative of any of the five counselors. Mr. Christianson's haphazard efforts to inform the eighth-grade students in his academy (Academy C) about high school choice, which is presented below, is more representative of the approach taken by most guidance counselors at IS 725.

Academy C housed all of the eighth-grade Spanish bilingual and ESL classes. Yet Mr. Christianson, a soft-spoken white man in his late thirties with graying, gel-spiked hair, did not speak or understand Spanish. He muddled through explanations of the application process with help from teachers, Spanish-speaking support staff, or Mr. Sanchez and Mr. Pedraza, the two bilingual guidance counselors at IS 725. Mr. Christianson started distributing high school applications to his seven eighth-grade classes the day they arrived, but he waited until the last three periods of the school day to do so. This was the first time all year that he had spoken formally to the eighth-grade students in Academy C about the choice process.

With seven minutes left before the end of period, Mr. Christianson knocked on the door of a bilingual math class in session and explained to the teacher that he had come to distribute the high school application. The twenty-five or so students in the class immediately began talking to each other in Spanish when Mr. Christianson entered the room. He tried to quiet them down but eventually started speaking over the din while the math teacher translated what he was saying into Spanish. Holding up the pile of applications, he said in English: "I am here to give out your applications. I'm going to give you until the end of November to fill it out and return it. Here are the important things: look at your address and telephone number. If it is not correct, correct it. Go see Ms. J [the school secretary]." The teacher translated this first comment but then gathered his books and walked out, leaving Mr. Christianson to fend for himself.

Mr. Christianson continued with his explanation (in English): "On the back of the application you list your choices. You don't have to put all twelve." A Dominican girl seated near the front of the class began yelling out phrases in Spanish in an unsuccessful attempt to translate. Picking up a *High School Directory*, Mr. Christianson asked if everybody had a copy. Despite a unanimous response of "No," he proceeded to tell them, "In the book they have the name of the school and the address. There are programs you have to apply to. On the back of the application there are boxes for the code. You put the program name, then the school name." When the bell rang signaling the end of the period, Mr. Christianson shouted out the final instructions. He attempted to incorporate some Spanish phrases into his explanations but the result was nonsensical:

> If you have questions, come to me but don't just show up. You need a pass. I won't see you without a pass. It is *muy importante* [very important] to choose a school *que me gusta* [that I like]. Not just because your friend goes there or your boyfriend or if it is close to your house but because it is something you are interested in.

As he exited the classroom, students swarmed Mr. Christianson, shouting and grabbing for their applications. After the mob subsided he remarked that he did not have sufficient time to review everything and wished the teacher had stayed to translate like he had agreed to do. Mr. Christianson then hurriedly made his way to the next class where a similar scene unfolded. These brief, poorly translated presentations constituted the only occasion in which Mr. Christianson explained the choice process to students in his academy. It was not surprising when over twenty of them still had not returned a completed application in December, nearly a month after the deadline.

Focus on Appeals and Application Deadline

For guidance counselors at IS 725, managing and containing the administrative demands associated with high school choice took precedence over counseling students and working with them to identify appropriate schools. In previous years the majority of students' appeals had been petitioned on the basis of a travel hardship. Therefore, in what appeared to be a strategic move to reduce the probability of future requests for appeals, guidance counselors emphasized school location as an essential criterion for students to consider when evaluating a school. Fewer requests for appeals also translated into less work on high school applications for guidance counselors and fewer hours spent responding to parents' and students' complaints.

The number of late applications submitted and the number of appeals requested were also the sole school-level measures that NYCDOE administrators could monitor from afar. NYCDOE has used the number of appeals to gauge public satisfaction with the choice process and has emphasized a decline in this figure in recent years as an indication of its steady improvement.[3] There were multiple reasons for guidance counselors to prioritize limiting the number of appeals.

Nearly every time guidance counselors spoke to students about high school choice, either individually or in groups, they mentioned the importance of considering school location and visiting websites to get estimated travel times. The guidance counselors made no effort to hide their desire to limit the number of appeals; on the contrary, they were forthright about their motivation for focusing on location. Ms. Perolli explained:

> Every year they put a school down and they don't go travel to see how far it is. And then when they get it, they decide it is too far . . . I tell them if you put it on there [the application], that means you want to go. I put it everywhere that they should watch travel time, call the school, take a Saturday [to make the trip]. I give them numbers to call and websites. Then the parents come in [to request an appeal].

Mr. Sanchez complained about the same issue directly to students and repeatedly instructed them to pay attention to where a school was located:

> There are always kids who put down Far Rockaway. Do you know where that is? It is all the way out there. It's still Queens, but it's like an hour and a half away . . . And the parents will say they didn't know, that they want to switch. "But you signed it," I tell them.

In contrast to their recurrent commentary about the importance of school location, the guidance counselors at IS 725 rarely discussed school performance as a factor to consider in school selection. The guidance counselors' lack of reference to traditional measures of school quality such as graduation rates, Regents passing rates, and college acceptances or even to newer metrics like the *Progress Report* grade was particularly notable in light of NYCDOE's substantial investment in creating publicly available accountability reports. Yet there were no incentives for guidance counselors or principals to ensure that their eighth-grade students applied to the highest performing schools to which they were eligible or, conversely, sanctions in cases of inadequate provision of information to high school applicants. Consequently, the middle school guidance counselors made a rational decision to highlight the aspect of the application process that had taken much of their time in years past: requests for appeals of high school assignments based on location. Despite this, nearly a hundred students from IS 725 still requested an appeal of their high school assignments the year of the study.

Beyond their almost single-minded attention to the issue of school location, the guidance counselors expended considerable energy reminding students to return their applications by the early December deadline. In fact, collecting applications was the only part of the high school choice process in which school personnel at IS 725 other than guidance counselors was directly involved. Assistant principals and paraprofessionals were enlisted to remind students to bring in their applications, to make phone calls to parents, and even to visit homes in search of overdue applications.

The guidance counselors' keen interest in meeting the deadline was not a coincidence: the principal received an email from NYCDOE headquarters after the submission deadline each year with a list of the students whose applications were missing from the system. Although none of the guidance counselors appeared particularly concerned about being reprimanded if he/she did not enter all the applications on time, they were aware that tardiness in completing this task was one of the few ways that NYCDOE administrators outside of the school building could track what they were doing. In fact, almost all the guidance counselors mentioned the district's ability to see when they had completed the data entry.

Starting in mid-November, nearly every response to inquiries about the status of the high school choice process related to guidance counselors' efforts to collect applications. As the deadline approached, some counselors seemed to value receiving completed applications over everything else. For example, in response to a question about what she would do if she saw that a student had listed very few schools on his/her application, Ms. Perolli unabashedly stated:

> I don't really do too much about that . . . I'm just happy they got the damn thing in. Because they send the principal a memo with the

names of the kids who don't have applications entered. That's another problem. So I just want to get them all in.

Guidance counselors utilized a number of tactics to guarantee students' prompt submission and to avoid an onslaught of applications in the final days before the deadline. Ms. Perolli, for one, intentionally misled students by telling them that the earlier they turned in their applications, the greater the likelihood that they would get their top choices. She was fully aware that the high school matching algorithm did not function that way, but she found this to be an effective method of encouraging students to return their applications early. Mr. Pedraza gave his students an earlier deadline, and then, starting the week before this fabricated deadline, he went to classrooms and the lunchroom on a daily basis to remind them to bring in their applications. As the deadline drew closer, guidance counselors made phone calls to parents to request that they deliver applications in person, and school attendance officers made home visits to collect applications as well.

Ultimately, some guidance counselors had more difficulty than others collecting completed applications by the deadline. Mr. Christianson, the non-Spanish-speaking counselor assigned to work with the Spanish-speaking students, had the fewest interactions with his students about choice; he was also the least successful at collecting applications. Two days prior to the start of Christmas vacation, when the online system was scheduled to shut down, twenty of the Spanish bilingual students in Academy C had not turned in their applications. Mr. Christianson spent the days in a frenzy running from classroom to classroom in search of students whose applications were missing. With the help of Mr. Sanchez and another bilingual paraprofessional, he attempted to call each student's parents to request oral permission to submit one or more schools in which the student had expressed interest. In many cases, however, the students did not know the name of any school, and Mr. Christianson resorted to entering only their local zoned school.

The local zoned high schools to which these students ended up "applying" were the same high schools to which they would have automatically been assigned in the absence of the choice policy. They were also some of the lowest performing schools in the city with graduation rates hovering around 50 percent. Although NYCDOE's statistics would count these students as having received their first choice of high school, there was no real choice involved. The way in which choice unfolded for this group of students—including the fact that almost no information about how to choose schools had been made available to them in a language they could understand—epitomizes the gap between the choice policy in theory and what occurs when it is implemented without guidelines, oversight, evaluation, and sufficient school-level resources.

COMPETING PRIORITIES AND THE POWER OF ACCOUNTABILITY

Accountability systems that use student performance on high-stakes tests and other evaluations to assess districts, schools, principals, teachers, and students are a defining feature of the educational landscape in the United States today. The accountability pressures that New York City schools are under have a distorting effect on counselors' practices. This is seen clearly in the marked differences between school personnel's responses to high school choice and to other district initiatives that are directly counted in district- and state-level accountability systems.

In contrast to the scant attention paid to the high school choice process, items linked to state and city accountability systems loomed large in the classrooms and hallways of IS 725. Those areas for which the school would be explicitly evaluated—namely, student performance on state standardized tests in English language arts and mathematics or parent response rates on the *Learning Environment Survey* (now called the *NYC School Survey*), which factors into the *Progress Report* grade—were given top billing. Moreover, the entire school community was engaged in working toward these goals, and considerable time, energy, and resources were dedicated to improving results from one year to the next. This meant that school personnel were urged to think and act creatively in order to encourage students and families to participate in related programs.

At the time of the study, IS 725 was classified as a School in Need of Improvement (SINI) by the New York State Education Department (NYSED). As a result, it was under intense pressure to raise student test scores on the state mathematics and English language arts examinations or face school closure, the removal of the principal, or mandatory staff changes. Consequently, the principal, assistant principals, and teachers demonstrated a laserlike focus on improving student test scores. This was evident in budgetary and staff allocations, in the topics emphasized at events for parents, and in casual conversations with school personnel.

New York City launched a multimillion-dollar accountability system during the 2007–2008 school year that operated in parallel to the state accountability and assessment systems linked to No Child Left Behind. An annual *Progress Report*, which combines measures of a school's success in accelerating student learning with other factors such as student, teacher, and parent satisfaction to determine a letter grade (A through F), is the cornerstone of New York City's system. Whereas schools that receive *Progress Report* grades of C, D, or F for multiple years are subject to NYCDOE interventions such as leadership change, restructuring, or even school closure, schools that earn high grades and meet their goals receive financial bonuses that could reach into the tens of thousands of dollars for principals and teachers (NYCDOE 2008).

Principal Robert Polo relayed the sense of urgency he felt to raise student scores and improve on accountability reports:

> It's tough this year . . . Because [last year] we met AYP [Adequate Yearly Progress], and we're trying to meet it again. It will be the first time the school meets it two years in a row. If we do [meet AYP two years in a row], we'll be off the [SINI] list and can't be put back for another two years . . . They can come in and close the school if we

don't meet AYP. They can send someone from the state, and if we don't make the changes, they'll just close us down . . . And this year everything is getting harder. The standards are changing, the tests are getting harder. So we really have to do it now.

Ms. Cutler, the assistant principal for Academy A and head of English language arts for the entire middle school, expressed comparable anxiety about meeting ever higher goals:

So last year we focused on the 3's and 4's [students who entered middle school at or above proficiency] and we did really well. I was actually shocked when we got the scores back. We improved like 15 or 18 percent. I don't know how we're going to do it again. It's a problem, figuring out how to make such big gains again.

The attention a policy, program, or practice received at IS 725 was directly correlated with the extent to which the district made explicit its expectations for implementation, inputs, and/or outcomes and how much these results counted for a school's *Progress Report* grade or other form of evaluation. This hierarchy of priorities revealed itself in multiple ways. The allocation of school-wide resources to different activities was one telling form of evidence. The energy and degree of creativity with which school personnel approached various tasks was another. For example, whereas guidance counselors were left basically alone to decide how to inform students and parents about high school choice, virtually every member of the school community was recruited to help improve parental response rates on the *Learning Environment Survey*. Both survey outcomes and response rates factored into the school's *Progress Report* grade, and the resources activated to increase parental response rates far exceeded those allocated to engage parents in the high school choice process. In addition, in contrast to its treatment of high school choice, when it came to the *Learning Environment Survey*, the school administration changed its outreach strategy from one year to the next in an attempt to experiment with better ways to reach families and encourage more responses.

Family engagement efforts related to high school choice were scaled back during the two years of the study. Over the course of this same two-year period, however, the principal at IS 725 directly responded to the poor parental response rate on the *Learning Environment Survey* in the first year (16 percent). He enlisted all five assistant principals in the task the following year and instituted a system of prizes for students whose parents turned in a completed survey. Through his active involvement and the resources he attached to this initiative, the principal clearly signaled to staff the importance of increasing parent response rate on the *Learning Environment Survey*. They, in turn, responded with significant investment in improving results.

The major shift that occurred in the school personnel's approach to distributing and collecting the *Learning Environment Survey* was a powerful sign of the school-wide commitment to improve response rates. As early as November, the principal instructed the school's parent coordinator to begin developing a revised outreach strategy. She did so even though surveys would not be distributed until late February. Ms. Lopez explained the changes they had implemented in their procedures when the survey effort was underway:

> We did not mail it home this year. We gave it out to students through their homeroom teachers. In past years they were mailed directly home and parents mailed them in. This year, the APs [assistant principals] all had boxes and the teachers were supposed to hand them back.

They also instituted a series of incentives for the first time that included giving points for a school-wide pizza party competition to students who turned in completed parent surveys. After an unsuccessful experience one year, the school personnel developed an entirely new tactic that required students', teachers', and assistant principals' participation. The principal and appointed staff raised the visibility of the *Learning Environment Survey* and made it a school-wide project using incentives, taking advantage of the school infrastructure, and dedicating additional human capital to the effort. During this same two-year period, high school choice received progressively less attention.

The school personnel's response to the *Learning Environment Survey* represents only one example of how accountability impacted school priorities. Evidence of its pervasive influence abounded. To help prepare students for state tests, the school relied heavily on the federally funded Supplementary Education Services (SES) program for additional support. The SES program offered low-income students enrolled in SINI schools the opportunity to receive up to thirty-five hours of individual or small-group test preparation from a variety of private tutoring companies. The staff at IS 725 expended tremendous energy publicizing the SES program and encouraging eligible families to enroll in it. During the first three months of the school year, Ms. Torres, the community outreach coordinator, together with Cristina Lopez, the parent coordinator, spent multiple days distributing SES information packets to eligible students, hosting information sessions for parents, organizing school-based fairs for SES providers, helping parents with registration forms, and calling and recruiting families who had enrolled students in SES in previous years to register again. In fact, at five school-wide parent events held at IS 725 over the course of the two years of the study, the principal made specific mention of SES. With the Spanish interpretation of Ms. Lopez, he repeatedly urged parents to sign their children up for tutoring services. Even at the high school choice workshop held for parents of eighth-grade students in the first year, Mr. Polo closed the event with a discussion about testing and enrolling in SES:

> I want to remind you of a few important things about eighth-graders . . . Now in order to graduate from eighth grade, students need a minimum of level two in reading and math . . . If you see a 65 or 70 [on their first report card], there is a chance that your child

won't pass, and we'll need to get him help now . . . If you didn't fill out forms for SES, you should . . . Only 10 percent of students who can participate have taken advantage.

He gave a similar speech at the "Back to School Night" for parents of seventh- and eighth-grade students in late September of the following year. In it Mr. Polo encouraged parents to monitor their children's report cards for early signs of failure. At the parent-teacher conferences held one afternoon in mid-November of that year, Ms. Lopez made multiple announcements over the loudspeaker in English and Spanish requesting that parents visit the cafeteria where she and other bilingual staff members would be sharing information about SES and assisting with enrollment in the program.

The principal used every occasion possible to emphasize to parents the importance of preparing students for state assessments and to advertise available academic supports—including at the fall parent high school application workshop. Conversely, the choice process was treated like a corollary to the core activities of the school. The principal never once made a public statement about high school choice, nor did he use events for seventh- and eighth-grade parents such as back to school night to share information about the choice process.

MATCHING EXPECTATIONS WITH OVERSIGHT AND INCENTIVES

School personnel's tepid engagement in high school choice activities at IS 725 shows the baselessness of district administrators' expectations of substantial school-based guidance on choice. By contrast, these same administrators, teachers, guidance and support staff worked vigorously to successfully implement policies and programs that "counted" in school evaluations. The clear discrepancies highlight the significance of requirements and oversight of school-level action in the present era of educational accountability. Compliance with NYCDOE policies is strongly influenced by the extent to which district goals and expectations are explicitly identified, compliance measured, and outcomes linked to rewards or punishments.

Schools like IS 725 that serve the most disadvantaged populations are being called on to furnish more intensive supports—academic and otherwise—to help all students reach academic proficiency and become "college and career ready." To do so, they require both resources and incentives. These same schools are often under the most intense scrutiny and pressure from local and state education authorities to improve student outcomes on standardized tests. As a result, they logically organize themselves and distribute resources to meet the benchmarks for which they will be rewarded and pay less attention to policies for which they will not be judged.

Given the context in which they were working, then, the guidance counselors at IS 725 acted rationally in response to symbolic and concrete stimuli indicating how and where their attention should be directed. Following the school leadership's prompts, they understood the high school choice process to be unrelated to the school's primary mission of improving student achievement and therefore of limited value. By excluding all aspects of the high school choice process from accountability measures and failing to provide guidelines or oversight of school-based implementation of the policy, NYCDOE also signaled to school personnel its relatively low status in the overall set of district objectives. Consequently, guidance counselors and school personnel treated the high school choice process as little more than a bureaucratic task. In doing so, an essential guidance component was lost. The chances that school choice could serve to correct a historic imbalance in students' access to high-quality educational opportunities was severely curtailed.

The power of accountability to influence schools represents both a danger and an opportunity. When No Child Left Behind (NCLB) was passed more than a decade ago, it established an unprecedented set of incentives and sanctions, in part, to increase focus on historically underserved or disadvantaged student populations. Since then, the ease with which such incentive structures can be distorted, manipulated, or produce perverse behaviors has been widely documented.[4] Holding schools responsible for assisting families with high school choice may be necessary to ensure that students receive a minimum amount of information, but such actions must be pursued judiciously. Recommendations for how districts can thoughtfully incorporate mechanisms to promote fidelity of policy implementation at the school level—or, at a minimum, encourage school personnel to engage in choice activities to the extent it has envisioned—are discussed at the end of the book. But first we turn to diverse students' and parents' narratives of participating in high school choice. Their accounts illustrate what a district's (and school's) failure to provide even basic information and guidance can mean for people's experiences with choice and students' ultimate high school assignments. The chapters that follow provide a closer look at how students and parents respond to the demands of the school choice process and reveal further cracks in NYCDOE's vision of the policy.

PART 2

STUDENTS AND FAMILIES

■■■

CHAPTER FOUR

Accompanied and Unaccompanied Minors

How Students Navigate
the School Choice Journey

A COMPLEX SERIES of overlapping, mutually reinforcing factors threaten the equity potential of high school choice in New York City. At the heart of the problem lies a set of inaccurate assumptions about students and families that inform the district's design and implementation of the choice policy. In part 1, I examined districtwide and school-based actions to inform, guide, and assist students and parents with the daunting task of choosing high schools in New York City. Students take center stage in the next two chapters. Eighth-grade students' narratives of learning about the choice process, identifying high school options, and, finally, making school choice decisions portray a wide range of experiences, understandings, resources, and support structures. The variation in their approaches, perspectives, and ultimate school assignments highlights the diversity that exists in students' responses to the demands of the choice policy and in their compliance with the New York City Department of Education's expectations.

Students' choice-making experiences, when viewed alongside their high school assignments, provide some of the strongest evidence of the incompatibility of equity and choice in New York City. Whereas the low-income Latino students at IS 725 seemed in large part to be lost in the school choice maze without direction or a discernible destination, the predominantly middle-class, Asian-origin students attending the magnet gifted and talented program at IS 725 actively engaged in school research and exploration. The consequences of the district's inaccurate assumptions of extensive student investment in searching for appropriate schools, highly involved parents, and substantive school-based guidance for all students are seen vividly in the haphazard choices and low performing high school placements of many of the low-income Latino youth. Conversely, the gifted and talented-track students, whose behaviors more closely approximated NYCDOE's vision, had vastly different school choice experiences and outcomes than their lower-income Latino peers. Their positive and, ultimately, successful experiences offer lessons about the specific resources, supports, structures, and activities that could help all students (and parents) make thoughtful, deliberate school choices.

Students in the gifted and talented track at IS 725 confronted the high school choice puzzle armed with a precise plan. They demonstrated a detailed understanding of the policy, possessed extensive knowledge about school offerings, used data to compare school performance, and relied on substantive input from family members, peers, and school personnel.

These elements functioned together as a powerful navigation tool or *institutional compass* that helped the gifted and talented-track students move through the complex school choice process. They also had a defined set of criteria for choosing schools that was informed and influenced by various people in their social worlds. In other words, they developed a *multiply reinforced orientation* to certain (typically high performing) high schools. Together, the combination of a well-developed approach to maneuvering through the high school choice labyrinth and a focused goal of obtaining admission to one of a select number of high performing high schools produced *strategic choice* behaviors. By contrast, the Latino students who described limited understanding or focus, lacked clear criteria for school selections, and chose high schools in relative isolation engaged in *passive choice.*

Evidence from student interviews belies simplistic conclusions that attribute patterns of *strategic* versus *passive* choosing solely to family background characteristics such as parental income and education or even to cultural norms and practices. One of the central arguments of *Unaccompanied Minors* is that the alignment of students' social spheres with regard to the task of choosing high schools is a major source of advantage for some choice participants (typically from higher socioeconomic backgrounds) or, on the other hand, a major disadvantage for students without it (often low-income and immigrant-origin). The patterns and themes that emerged in student interviews illuminated the exponential power of receiving consistent, reinforced messages from peers, family members, and school personnel in terms of generating an institutional compass, making informed school choices, and developing research and decision-making skills generally. The interviews also revealed some of the consequences of district-level policies that fail to put in place a robust infrastructure to assist students who do not have access to similarly integrated support systems. These ideas, processes, and outcomes will be discussed in greater depth in the next chapter.

This chapter explores how four separate factors—the role of peers, school-based information sources, school selection criteria, and family member involvement contributed to students' dramatically different forms of engagement in high school choice. Forty-six eighth-grade students from IS 725 were interviewed, and consistent patterns were found among students in four distinct groups: first- and second-generation children of East and South Asian immigrants in the gifted and talented track; high performing first- and second-generation Latino students in the honors and regular tracks; low performing second- and third-generation Latino and African American students in the regular track; and recent immigrants from the Dominican Republic, Ecuador, and Mexico in the Spanish bilingual track. When it came to the role of family members in students' school search and decision-making processes, however, only three student groupings were relevant: first- and second-generation children of Latin American immigrants (in the honors, regular, and bilingual tracks); children of East and South Asian immigrants (in the gifted and talented track); and African American and third-generation or higher students (in the regular track).[1]

THE ROLE OF PEERS IN HIGH SCHOOL SELECTIONS

The important role that peers play in adolescents' academic and social lives has been well established in the research literature.[2] In light of the considerable evidence regarding peer influences, it was not surprising that peer influence emerged as a dominant theme in students' narratives of their high school choice experiences.

Gifted and Talented-Track Students

Peers played a prominent and versatile role in the school search and decision-making processes of the mostly Asian middle-class students in the gifted and talented track. Their primary function was to supply information about specific high schools, dates for open houses and choice events, and procedures related to the high school application itself. If a student was the first in his/her family to attend high school in New York City, he/she was particularly dependent upon peers and classmates whose older siblings had already been through the choice process.

A powerful set of shared norms about how to go about choosing high schools operated within the gifted and talented classroom. These norms appeared to strongly influence students' search behaviors, the schools they would and would not consider, and the order in which they listed high schools on their application forms. In fact, these students frequently recounted engaging in identical search activities—often together—consulting the same set of information sources and having the same high school preferences. The gifted and talented students' sense of shared expectations and focus was exemplified in three ways: their uniform research strategies, a similar prioritization of high schools on the final application, and their treatment of the entire process as a collaborative venture. First, when recounting the activities they engaged in prior to completing the application form, many of the gifted and talented interview participants spoke as if they were following the steps of some widely known rulebook that all of their friends and classmates possessed. This was the common *institutional compass*—a precise approach to finding their way through the high school choice labyrinth—being put to use. Their search strategy included attending at least one high school fair and multiple high school open houses, searching online for information about a high school's graduation rates, college acceptances, Regents passing rates, and SAT scores, and asking relatives, friends, teachers, and other adults what they knew about different schools. Perhaps most importantly, this also included preparing for and taking the specialized high school admissions test.

Next, their explanations of the high schools to which they ultimately decided to apply and in what order highlighted the consistency of their goals and the existence of a strong normative undercurrent. Because nearly every student in the gifted and talented track took the specialized high school admissions test, those schools were most frequently named at the top of their lists. In response to a question about the order in which she put the high schools on her application, Asma, a second-generation Indian student explained: "Oh, regular, like everyone put. Because obviously it's Specialized High School 1, Specialized High School 2, and Specialized High School 3.[3] Those are the three major ones." Seema, the U.S.-born daughter of Pakistani immigrants, further described the hierarchy of high schools that was well known by her classmates: "Because at first you don't really pay attention to schools like Specialized High School 3 or Specialized High

School 2 . . . you are aiming at Specialized High School 1 and everything . . . Because they say that Specialized High School 1 is like the best high school there is . . . So everybody is going to aim for Specialized High School 1 then."

Students who took the specialized test also had the opportunity to apply to twelve additional high schools, so a similarly homogeneous pattern was seen in how the gifted and talented track students ranked their "nonspecialized" high schools. Seema discussed how she and her friends ordered their preferences:

> Yeah, because they [her classmates] saw that when the [eligibility] requirements has [sic] to be like 95 to 100 or 98 to 100 and all of us like fell into that . . . For public [nonspecialized] high schools, it's mostly because most kids in our class always put Thompson High School first because it was apparent, but I think the story was that Thompson High School was supposed to be a specialized school . . . So we had Thompson High School, Smith High School, Johnson High School, um, Parker High School . . .

Students in the gifted and talented class were all keenly aware of which schools were desirable or even acceptable in the eyes of their classmates. Therefore, when one student deviated from the class norm by ranking Specialized High School 2 before Specialized High School 1, she described feeling like "an outsider."

The fact that a number of students in the gifted and talented track discussed the high school choice process as a collective undertaking constituted a final distinguishing feature of their experiences and approach. Like students from across IS 725, gifted and talented-track students attempted to coordinate their lists with friends in an effort to avoid being "alone." However, the coordination did not end there. These students attended open houses and high school fairs together, they spoke to one another's older siblings about their high school experiences, and perhaps most importantly, they understood it as a joint endeavor in which every additional piece of information obtained was communal property.

As Seema recounted: "She [the guidance counselor] said if you have any questions you can come to my office. And every week or two a kid would go then he'd tell us like, 'She said this, this, be aware of this.'"

In the end, the gifted and talented-track students understood themselves to be a unit—one that was separate and distinct from the rest of the eighth-graders in the school. Their reliance on one another for a variety of functions reflected this. Asma's comment demonstrates this shared perception: "But, like, I know in some other classes they didn't really care [about high school]. They would just prefer to go to their zoned school and they really didn't care. But for us, like, we knew where we wanted to go and we wanted to go to a good high school." Asma drew a firm line between the gifted and talented-track students and everyone else. In reality, the differences were not always as stark.

High Performing Latino Students

The high performing Latino students in both honors and regular-track classes similarly relied on their peers as sources of information. However, their peers often had limited information or generic knowledge about schools, and they conducted less rigorous investigations on their own than the gifted and talented-track students. Moreover, the clear consensus among gifted and talented students about what were considered appropriate high school selections, or their *multiply reinforced orientation* toward high schools with specific academic qualities, was absent among high performing students in both honors and regular-track classes.

When the high performing Latino students discussed their peers' involvement in their high school choices, they described having brief conversations about the schools to which they were applying and why. They were interested in finding "good" high schools, and they exchanged tips about school options whenever possible. Maristela, the eldest daughter of Salvadoran immigrants, recounted how she and her friends discussed high school choice: "We talked about like, what schools we would go to . . . if they are . . . if they [friends] recommend [the schools] to us also . . . what schools we chose, how's the criteria [eligibility requirements], what you want to learn." Other students mentioned analogous discussions with friends and classmates that focused on identifying schools where there are "no bad kids" and "you have to have good grades to make it to the school."

High performing Latino students also found their friends and classmates to be important sources of support in making decisions about high schools. For many of them, this support was missing at home. Emilio, the eldest of five children born to poor, Mexican immigrant parents who themselves had not attended high school, explained: "Another friend of mine, he's an eighth-grader and told me to choose, um, I should choose uh, a high schools that would benefit me later on in life and stuff." Perhaps because so few of these students reported attending any high school fairs or open houses, none of them mentioned engaging in any concrete school search activities jointly with their peers.

Finally, although there was no evidence of shared standards for how to choose high schools among high performing students, a number of them ended up applying to the same schools. In fact, six students in one of the honors classes were matched to the same Manhattan high school. This result was notable because one of the high performing students spoke excitedly about his and five other of his friends having been assigned this school. However, the school had a four-year graduation rate below 65 percent the prior year. Thus, for some high performing Latino students, peer influences did not always lead to academically beneficial results: friends and classmates might encourage one another to apply to high schools they erroneously perceived as high performing based on limited knowledge of the schools.

Lower Performing Students

Peers played a significantly more limited role in the high school choice experiences of lower performing students than they did for gifted and talented-track and high performing students. While nearly 75 percent of the average and low performing students mentioned some form of peer involvement in the course of their interviews, peers contributed little more than basic information or pressure to apply to certain schools and avoid others. For example, multiple students discussed hearing about some of the schools to which they ended up applying from friends and classmates. When pressed to elaborate on what they actually learned about a school from their friends, however, it became evident that peers provided few details beyond what could be found in the directory—location, theme, size, and if applicable, eligibility criteria. Moreover, in contrast to gifted and talented students who used peer recommendations to prompt independent research about a school, average and low performing students were content with knowing that other friends or classmates had put a school on their applications before including it on their own. In fact, the importance of applying to the same school as one's friends came up more frequently in interviews with these students than with any other group. For them, coordinating applications with friends was unrelated to conforming to certain norms or ensuring assignment to a high-quality high school. Instead, it stemmed directly from their fears of not knowing anyone else at the school.

Crystal's comment captures this perspective: "Because, some people, they don't like going to schools where they know none of their friends are going so that's how my friends influenced me 'cause I don't like being the only one that goes to a school." In sum, although peers were a salient factor in low-performing students' narratives of choosing high schools, they did not serve as a source of instrumental information about how to effectively navigate the process or identify appropriate schools based on school quality or other metrics. Peers, friends, and classmates offered little more to low performers than superficial knowledge about schools and a sense of security that one would not be alone in applying to specific ones.

SCHOOL PERSONNEL INVOLVEMENT

Limited research exists on the ways in which school choice participants use school-based information sources. While studies have shown that lower income, less educated, and minority parents tend to rely more on school-based sources of information than higher income, higher educated, and white parents, data on parents' actual interactions with school personnel and their consumption of the choice materials that schools produce are relatively scarce.[4] Even less is known about students' use of information furnished by schools.

A majority of students at IS 725, regardless of academic track or achievement, discussed peers in some capacity during the course of their interviews. Considerably fewer students cited school personnel or school-based events as providing help and information about choosing high schools. More specifically, nearly all the gifted and talented-track students and most of the recent immigrant Latino students in bilingual classes named school personnel as contributing to their choice decisions. Fewer than half of the high performing Latino students or low performing students made reference to receiving assistance from teachers, guidance counselors, or school staff. Although school personnel were featured prominently in both gifted and talented and recent immigrant students' accounts, two very distinct patterns emerged. The information and opinions furnished by school guidance counselors or teachers served to reinforce gifted and talented students' own knowledge and ideas generated through independent research and family discussions. Conversely, the messages that recent immigrant students received from teachers about high schools was often their sole source of information.

Gifted and Talented-Track Students

Gifted and talented-track students relied on guidance counselors and teachers to augment their independent information-gathering efforts. Before consulting with school personnel, they identified and researched schools and began to formulate a list of schools that met their academic criteria and best matched their skills and interests. School-based information served to strengthen and reinforce the messages and resources that they had already received from peers and family members. Some gifted and talented students mentioned instances when teachers initiated discussion about the schools they were considering, but the role of school personnel came up almost universally in the context of students describing how they sought out additional advice or clarification. Monisha, the U.S.-born daughter of Indian immigrant parents, described speaking privately with her guidance counselor about high schools during the parent-teacher conference. Laxmi, another Indian-origin student in the gifted and talented track, set up a special time for her and her mother to meet with the guidance counselor to discuss high school options. Other students visited the guidance counselor or teachers during their lunch period to talk about high schools, and those students who participated in an afterschool test-preparation program put on by IS 725 for the specialized high school admissions exam (five of the interviewees in total) all mentioned getting useful tips about which high schools to consider from the teacher who led the program.

The information that gifted and talented-track students gleaned or requested from school personnel relating to the high school application fell into one of four categories. In most cases, students sought feedback from their guidance counselor or teacher about the schools in which they were already interested. Generally, they wanted to know if the school was academically rigorous enough for them, if it was safe, and it if had a good "reputation." Students also frequently requested names of other schools they might have overlooked that would also match their academic and thematic/career requirements. Guidance counselors were consulted about choice policy guidelines, including their recommendation for the minimum number of high schools to list in order to avoid the supplementary round. Finally, students described having conversations with teachers about the experience of transitioning to high school and what would be expected of them. Asma's description of her interactions with the guidance counselor exemplified the role that school personnel played for many of the gifted and talented students:

> Well, I talked to her [the guidance counselor], um, like at lunch . . . Or I'd go before school and she'd tell me about what high schools were good and stuff. There was [sic] parent-teacher conferences, and I'd go to talk to her . . . She was really helpful, she knew a lot about the high schools and like how many people were there and like transportation . . . She thought what I chose was really good, like because of my average and what I got in each class.

Gifted and talented-track students were able to depend on school personnel to provide complementary information, feedback, and overall guidance when making high school choices. As a result of their own pursuit of additional support, these students received personalized recommendations from school personnel about how to make sensible and appropriate choices given their interests and academic record. Efforts to use school-based resources to garner concrete information and suggestions were consistent with the gifted and talented-track students' behaviors overall: they asked detailed questions about each school's academic performance and other characteristics to see if it aligned with their interests and goals.

High Performing Latino Students

School personnel played a substantially less prominent and instrumental role in high performing Latino students' search for high schools. Only half of the eight students in this category referenced school-based information sources even once during the course of the interview. Those students who did mention school personnel largely described receiving operational information about application due dates and city-wide events. Emilio, for example, explained that teachers and guidance counselors merely served to distribute the *High School Directory* and the application form. When probed if they offered any instructions or advice, Emilio noted, "[They told us to] look over it [the directory] over the summer and choose wisely . . . We have to read, study it over, and choose our high schools that we wanted to apply for. Then in eighth grade they gave us a high school application paper and then we fill it out, and we hand it in."

In a few instances, high performing Latino students described seeking out guidance counselors' or teachers' advice about which high schools to consider in a fashion similar to the gifted and talented-track students. Yet these random moments of guidance were insufficient to stimulate the development of a coherent orientation and corresponding strategy for securing high-quality high school placements. As a result, without a consistent alignment between home and school messages promoting a common goal, the potential impact of school personnel's direction toward higher quality high schools was severely diluted.

Lower Performing Students

Interviews with low performing students in the regular track shed light on the value of building formal guidance structures to support eighth-grade students' high school choices. The weekly "mandated" counseling sessions that some of these students were required to attend served as a built-in opportunity for them to receive personalized guidance and support about high schools. Every regular-track student interviewed who was required to meet weekly with his/her guidance counselor for "mandated counseling" (based on psychological or other assessments), nine in total, described having conversations about high schools during this scheduled meeting time.

Manny, the U.S.-born son of Peruvian immigrants, developed a close, personal relationship with his guidance counselor over the course of his mandated counseling sessions. This led to his relying on her for advice about high schools. When his initial application included only one high school—a failing zoned school in the neighborhood—his counselor, Ms. Brown, pushed him to consider alternatives: "She told me, 'No, you should just put more down just in case and you could have better options.' So, like, I trust Ms. Brown because I've been talking to her for a while and stuff. So I was like, if she thinks that's what I should do, I should do that." Manny ultimately ended up applying to five different schools. Establishing a dedicated time and space for students to discuss the complicated high school choice process with a counselor or other advisor could yield more informed and potentially more beneficial choices. At a minimum, structured time for conversations about high school choice might help direct students away from low performing high schools or expand their choice sets.

Recent Immigrant Students

School personnel played a particularly important role in recent immigrant students' high school selections. No other forms of instrumental support or sources of information were present in these students' lives. Consequently, the impact and significance of teachers' and, in rare instances, guidance counselors' involvement were elevated. In other words, school personnel's commentary, which generally took the form of broad recommendations about which schools would be appropriate for all bilingual students, by default became the unofficial rules that many recent immigrant students followed. On one hand, recent immigrant students benefited from the fact that their teachers appeared to be more likely than those teaching students in the regular and honors tracks to initiate discussions about high school. On the other hand, the information they did receive was in no way personalized to their particular interests, skills, or needs (other than language). Instead, teachers named a finite number of schools—international high schools (dedicated exclusively to serving recent immigrants) and zoned high schools—that they believed to be suitable options for students in bilingual education classes. To fill the information and instruction void, first-generation immigrant students depended heavily on teachers' broad suggestions about a predetermined group of schools. As a result, their applications tended to be virtually identical, including only the international high schools and/or the large zoned high schools in their neighborhoods that housed bilingual education programs.

Take the case of Julisa, a recently arrived immigrant student from the Dominican Republic. Her account of how she learned about the high school choice process and the information provided by her teachers was representative of those given by nearly every recent immigrant student interviewed:

> Really, my teachers instructed me . . . I don't know one of their names, but Mr. González helped a lot . . . He told me which schools to pick, how to do it . . . He recommended [name of school], the international one because it is like for recently arrived students. And [name of school] and I think that's it, nothing else. [translated from Spanish by the author]

The fact that Julisa could not even remember the name of one of the teachers she cited as helping her with high school selections indicates the lack of relational support that she (and many of her recent immigrant classmates) received. However, with no alternatives, these students seized any bit of information they could from school personnel to point them in the direction of sanctioned high schools. The reality of how these recently arrived immigrant students engaged in "choice" was a far cry from what NYCDOE administrators envisioned.

SCHOOL SELECTION CRITERIA

The rich literature on parents' reasons for choosing schools shows that all parents, regardless of socioeconomic status or racial/ethnic background, consistently name academic factors.[5] Discipline/safety, transportation/proximity, and religion/values are other frequently cited explanations. Students' preferences prior to college-going age, on the other hand, have received almost no scholarly attention.[6]

Gifted and Talented-Track Students

Without exception, gifted and talented-track students laid out a nearly identical rationale for winnowing the seven hundred possibilities to a maximum of twelve schools. Aside from specialized high schools that use an exam score as the sole admissions criterion, for a school to even merit consideration by gifted and talented students, it had to restrict admission to students who had earned a minimum of an 85 in all four core seventh-grade classes (English language arts, math, social studies, and science) and scored at or above proficiency ("level three") on state tests. Once meeting this minimum threshold, students also considered the number of advanced placement courses offered, opportunities to earn college credits, the selectivity of colleges and universities that graduates attended, and SAT and Regents exam scores. Only after these "academic" criteria were satisfied would gifted and talented students begin to consider a school's career focus or theme. Last, they factored in how popular a school was (how many applicants it had in previous years) and what classmates and other people said about the school's reputation. Gifted and talented-track students favored those schools that were highly competitive, had many more applicants than available spots, and had a "good" reputation. Monisha summarized the approach taken by most of her classmates in the gifted and talented track:

> Some of the most popular schools are Thompson High School and Specialized High School 1. So I started off with that first and then basically [looked at] the programs they offered and also how many people get accepted and how many people apply. So the ones that people apply more to, it's like, I would assume that more people would go there because it's a better school. And then also the *Progress Report* ratings.

High Performing Latino Students

High performing Latino students repeatedly expressed their desire to attend "good" high schools. Yet they did not search for a range of data points to determine whether a school met their academic requirements like their counterparts in the gifted and talented track. Instead, these students relied on only one indicator before deciding that a school passed muster. The admissions criteria that were provided for each school in the directory were the decisive academic factors. Jordan, the U.S.-born son of Mexican immigrant parents in one of the honors classes, described his logic for selecting schools:

> I picked most of the top schools, so not top but like smart schools. Like Williams High School, it was my number one. I read in the book [*High School Directory*]; it said you needed a 90 average, which was like pretty good . . . in the book it says like standards they want. For example, 90 average, the programs in it, all that stuff . . . [What is] important to me are the standards of the school. If I have a 70 average I am not going to go to a 90 average school because I am not going to, like, make it. So I thought to myself, I have a good average to get into a good school.

Because high performing students considered fewer academic features of a school, they used career and thematic focus more frequently than gifted and talented-track students to narrow down the large number of options available. Additionally, they mentioned sports, afterschool activities, and knowing people who attended or were applying to the school as important considerations. Their more superficial or *passive* engagement in the process of identifying appropriate high schools overall was apparent in their more limited search for data on schools' academic performance.

Lower Performing Students

In many ways, low performing students faced the most formidable challenge choosing high schools. Their grades prevented them from applying to the most competitive high schools in the city, so unlike high performing students, they could not use admissions criteria to identify possible options and reduce the field. Since the majority of schools in New York City do not have selective admissions criteria, regular track students were left with hundreds of possibilities through which to wade. In response, they depended on two main features of a school: location and theme/career. In some cases they also considered reputation and friends' and siblings' attendance.

Nearly one-third of the lower performing students mentioned academic qualities in the course of their interviews. However, they did so to explain that they only checked a school's academic requirements in order to establish whether their grades qualified (and would not exclude) them for admission. Most of these students restricted their geographic parameters to the borough of Queens; sometimes, they expanded the parameters to include schools in Manhattan. Setting geographic limits allowed them to bypass the sections of the *High School Directory* dedicated to the other three (or four) boroughs and concentrate on identifying high schools with curricular or career foci related to their interests. Lower performing students varied in terms of the importance they placed on applying to the same schools as friends, attending the same school as siblings, or the weight they gave to location versus career focus, but these four considerations were of primary import.

Recent Immigrant Students

The recent immigrant students' reports about school selection criteria were markedly different from those of the rest of their peers at IS 725. Their inability to name concrete details about any of the schools to which they applied and near universal reference to teachers' recommendations as the major reason for listing a school provided further evidence of their shallow knowledge of schools and limited comprehension of the application process overall.

Significantly, when recent immigrant students did reveal some familiarity with specific high schools, it was almost always when citing neighborhood zoned high schools that they wanted to avoid because of safety fears, gangs, and negative rumors. Milton, an immigrant student from Ecuador, put it succinctly when asked whether he was putting down his zoned high school: "No [I am not putting down my zoned high school], because they are going to close it and it is a bad school, they say. Everyone says that it is a bad school, the people hanging around outside, the students" [translated from Spanish by the author]. For Milton and many other students—recent immigrant and U.S.-born alike, awareness of schools to avoid or schools to pursue did not necessarily translate into actions that would best position them to realize their high school placement goals. Lacking focus, guidance, information, and a basic understanding of how to use the choice process to their advantage, many students—Milton among them—were ultimately assigned to the same low performing neighborhood high schools they would have attended if the choice policy weren't in place.

FAMILY INVOLVEMENT

Family member involvement in students' choices constitutes the final and in many ways most significant piece of the puzzle explaining differences in their high school choice experiences in New York City. The role that parents and other family members played in students' high school selections represents a departure from the patterns delineated earlier in the chapter. Academic track/achievement was the most salient grouping category for identifying differences in how peers and school personnel impacted students' school selections and in their school selection criteria. However, parents' nativity and countries of origin proved to be the main determinant of students' reports of family involvement in high school choice. The family members' distinct degrees and forms of involvement most vividly displayed the challenges associated with being a child of low-income Latin American immigrant parents when it came to choosing high schools. Regardless of a student's academic track, achievement level, nativity, or country of origin, if a student interviewee was born to an immigrant mother from Mexico, Ecuador, the Dominican Republic, or other parts of Latin America, he/she was considerably less likely to report receiving any home-based support in identifying schools and completing the application than Asian-origin gifted and talented-track students, African American, or third-generation-plus students.

Students described a range of parental behaviors that could be classified into four categories: instrumental involvement, directive involvement, symbolic involvement, and limited involvement. Parents who searched independently for information about schools; activated their social networks to request advice and suggestions from friends, colleagues, family members, or neighbors; and spent time working with their children to determine appropriate school options engaged in *instrumental involvement. Directive parent involvement* consisted of parents explicitly instructing students about which schools they could and could not apply to, (although instructions were not always accompanied by oversight and enforcement). *Symbolic involvement* was exhibited in the form of encouraging words about school generally and exhortations to do well in school or to "choose wisely." This most often occurred in the absence of concrete ideas or supports for identifying and choosing acceptable schools. Finally, the classification of *limited involvement* was applied to cases where students' references to parents were restricted to their having signed the application or asking if they had turned it in on time; examples of limited involvement could also include parents who made generalized, nondirective statements about schools. Other family members, particularly siblings but also aunts, uncles, grandparents, and cousins, played a variety of roles spanning from gatekeeper (ensuring that students did not apply to "bad schools") to financial supporter (paying for classes to prepare for the specialized high school admissions test).

Gifted and Talented-Track Students

Students in the gifted and talented track reported the greatest amount of parent and family participation in high school choice, and they described substantial *instrumental* and *directive involvement*. Their parents dedicated days and evenings to learning about schooling options and determining how to best position their children for admission to competitive high schools. Beyond accompanying their children to high school fairs, open houses, and meetings with guidance counselors, gifted and talented-track students described parents calling high schools on their own, speaking with coworkers and friends, and conducting Internet research to find out specific details about schools, mostly related to their academic outcomes. Their parents also had concrete ideas about which schools were acceptable. In some cases, parents' opinions conflicted with their children's. Monisha's description of her mother's role was typical of the gifted and talented students' accounts:

> Well, she [my mother] also came to open houses, and she gave her opinion on which schools were better . . . She liked Specialized High School 1 and Thompson High School the best, but she liked Roberts High School too because it was smaller and is situated inside Community College and so it's like a more open environment . . . The class sizes were smaller so there was [*sic*] more teachers and she liked that too. But she liked Specialized High School 1 . . . I wanted to go to fashion designing school too. My mom said no. And I had all auditions for that but then my mom didn't let me go to the audition. She wants me to be a doctor . . .

Siblings, cousins, and other relatives were also influential figures in gifted and talented-track students' choice decisions. Older siblings and cousins who had experience choosing high schools offered advice and opinions, connected students to their friends in different high schools, and generally served as sounding boards for anxious eighth-graders awaiting their results. In the case of Salman, a second-generation Bangladeshi student, an uncle covered the cost of a preparatory class in order to improve his chances of scoring high enough on the Specialized High School Admissions Test (SHSAT) to be admitted to Stuyvesant, which his cousin had attended. For Asma, an older sister guided her through the process and helped in multiple ways:

> Another person [who helped me] would be my sister because she knew it from the top of her head, like, she already had a plan for me what high schools I would apply to. So, and then she told me, "Do you have this down?" "Do you have this down?" "Do you have this school down?" And then she actually knew a lot because . . . from her middle school a lot of friends went to different high schools and she kept in contact with them and she knew a lot about their schools and . . . how good it was.

African American and Third-Generation or Higher Students

African American and third-generation-plus students referenced parents and family members with almost the same frequency as Asian-origin students in the gifted and talented track. However, the nature of their family members' involvement was quite different. African American and third-generation-plus parents' participation in the choice process was almost exclusively confined to the realm of *directive involvement*. Students rarely recounted examples where parents conducted independent research to obtain school-related data; instead, they spoke of receiving instructions about which "good" schools to apply to and which "bad" schools to avoid based on parents' (often outdated) knowledge of schools from other relatives, older children's experiences, and their own time in high school in New York City. Moreover, students cited few instances in which they spoke with parents at length about what they were interested in studying, how to evaluate schools, and which school characteristics would best fit their skills, personalities, and preferences.

African American and third-generation-plus students' accounts of their parents' school preferences did not appear to deviate significantly from what children of Latin American immigrants reported about their parents. Both sets of parents expressed a desire for their children to stay close to home and avoid schools with safety issues. However, African American and third-generation or higher parents were operating from a more solid base of information about how the school system functioned as a whole, and they were more aware of the universe of possibilities across the city due to personal or familial experiences with the education system. As a result, their children's narratives relayed a greater parental presence in their application process even if parents did not furnish additional instrumental information about schools.

Siblings and relatives were also directly involved in the African American and third-generation-plus students' high school choices. However, unlike the Asian-origin gifted and talented-track students' accounts in which family members encouraged them to pursue only the most rigorous, competitive, and high performing schools, family members of African American/third-generation-plus eighth-graders did not exclusively steer them toward safe, high performing schools. Whereas some students recalled siblings warning them against specific schools (usually their local zoned high schools) in which they themselves had had unpleasant experiences or about which they had heard negative reports, others described feeling pressured or strongly encouraged by siblings to attend the same high school even if it was low performing or dangerous. Similar patterns were observed in the roles of siblings for Latino, immigrant-origin students.

In spite of African American and third-generation-plus parents' relatively greater visibility throughout the high school choice process, at least compared to Latin American immigrant parents, the majority of these students relayed an overall sense of being singularly responsible for their own choices. In some cases, these students listed certain schools on their applications even after their parents had expressed disapproval because parents did not always follow through with oversight after an initial or brief conversation about high schools. This theme of students being left alone to complete the high school application was even more prominent in interviews with children of Latin American immigrants.

Children of Low-Income Latin American Immigrants

Children of low-income immigrants from Mexico, Ecuador, the Dominican Republic, and other parts of Latin America offered a uniform picture of parents who had minimal understanding of the high school choice process itself or the high school options that existed across the city. They were also ignorant of what was expected of them and their eighth-grade students. These students' references to parent participation in high school choice fell overwhelmingly into the category of *limited involvement*. There were minor differences, depending on their parents' time in the U.S. and if the student was the first in the family to participate in high school choice. These parents' behaviors were consistent with what has been well documented in the research literature with regard to the ways in which Latin American immigrant parents with limited education tend to support their children's education: through encouragement, home-based activities, and a focus on cultivating their children's moral development. Conversely, academic matters tend to be left to education professionals who are seen as better trained to resolve school-related issues.[7]

The traditional parental involvement practices of low-income Latin American immigrants played out in various ways in the context of high school choice in New York City. For example, Maribel, a high performing Dominican-born student and only child, described her mother's limited comprehension of the choice process. Her response to a standard interview question about parents' roles and understanding of high school choice was representative of what many other children of Latin American immigrants expressed:

> Um, she knows that you're supposed to put the school that you want to go to and if they accept you they tell you in April . . . She doesn't know that much. She only knows that you put [the schools] . . . and then they tell you if you are accepted. 'Cause she only cares, like, if where you want to go, that's where [they] will accept you.

In a few instances, students mentioned that their Latin American immigrant parents had independently inquired about high schools or shared unsolicited opinions. Inquiries tended to be related to administrative aspects of the process such as when the application was due and whether or not the student had submitted the application on time. These parents were often singularly focused on ensuring that their child was following the school rules regarding the application procedures. This orientation corresponds to what has been previously found in terms of low-income Latin American immigrants' conception of their principal role as moral educators who must teach their children to be respectful and comply with behavioral standards, customs, and traditions.[8]

Latino students reported that their parents were most concerned about a school's safety and distance from home. However, their parents' knowledge about schools was very basic and was usually based on hearsay and rumors from friends and neighbors about the local zoned high schools. When a student had an older sibling attending high school, his/her parents nearly always expressed a preference that he/she attend the same school, regardless of what the student wanted or had heard about its safety and academic quality. The only exceptions to this pattern were when an older child had dropped out of high school; then, parents would advise against applying there.

Although different in nature from *limited involvement*, the parents who engaged in forms of *symbolic involvement* offered few opinions or tools that could be applied in the context of high school choice either. Symbolic involvement was a unique aspect of some Latin American immigrant parents' participation in their children's choice experiences. Consonant with anthropological studies that have highlighted the significance of *consejos* or advice from elders as part of the child socialization process in Mexican and other Latin American cultures, students described receiving encouragement from parents to do well academically and choose "wisely."[9] Jordan, the high performing son of Mexican immigrants in the honors track, recounted his parents' role in the following way: "They are like, 'Just, just get into a good school, pass, do, like, your hardest, try your best.'" When asked if his parents knew how to get into a "good" school, he replied, "I have no idea; I don't think so." In the case of Jasmin, another second-generation, high performing Dominican student, both parents offered separate but similarly symbolic forms of encouragement:

> She [my mother] was like, "Don't choose a school that's far away. Choose something that you like and something that'll be a comfort to you." My dad, he's like, "Choose a school that is going to benefit you in the future, like something you like."

The support, motivation, and encouragement these students received from their parents did not furnish them with concrete information about schools or tactical strategies to improve their chances of being accepted to their top choices. Furthermore, the rare exchanges that did take place between eighth-graders and their Latin American immigrant parents were devoid of discussion about students' educational interests or aspirations. As a result, these students were generally left to their own devices to determine which high schools to apply to, or they had to seek out advice from other sources such as school personnel, friends, or other family members.

Many children of Latin American immigrants turned to older siblings and cousins with experience in New York City high schools for assistance choosing schools. The case of Estafani, a recently arrived immigrant student from the Dominican Republic, is illustrative of the role of siblings. Her desire to attend the same school as her older brother and sister also reflects the strong value of familism found to exist in many Latin American cultures.[10] She explained her decision to only list the failing local zoned high school and her mother's support of her decision:

> Well, first of all . . . my sister always told me to pick [local zoned high school] because that way they [my siblings] could help me . . .

Although people have always told me that [school name] is bad. It's a bad school. No, [I only put] that one. Because that's the one that was my zoned school . . . [My mom] said that it was fine. Because since . . . my brother is there and my other siblings have always been good in that school. [translated from Spanish by the author]

Jordan espoused a similar perspective. He was aware that the local zoned high school from which his brother just barely graduated had a notorious reputation for low performance and gang violence. And despite his expressed desire to attend a "smart school" that corresponded to his high grades, in the end Jordan included the zoned high school on his application. He did so because he felt confident he would be able to graduate from the school like his brother and saw it as a last resort:

Um, my brother helped out a bit. He's like, just go to that school. You could pick [the local zoned high school where his brother went] if you want, it's not that great but you know . . . Yeah, that's the only thing, there are a lot of bad kids . . . I put it . . . Since my brother graduated there, why not me? If he could do it, I could do it.

When Jordan was eventually matched to this high school, he was deeply disappointed and immediately submitted a request for an appeal. In August, he was despondent when his appeal request was denied by NYCDOE. His parents could not understand his disappointment since the local zoned high school was around the corner from his house and his brother had eventually earned his diploma after five years.

In the absence of informed and involved parents, more students in the Latin American immigrant-origin sample discussed sibling involvement than any other group. Although these siblings did not provide the kind of instrumental, detailed, data-driven information that Asian-origin students reported getting from their family members, older siblings often helped direct them away from potentially poor-quality high schools and into preferable, higher performing ones. Andrea, a second-generation Colombian student and the youngest of three girls, explained how her sisters monitored her application:

> My sisters . . . they did it. They all went through it so they taught me, they were telling me what to pick and all of that . . . They didn't want me to go to [names three low performing zoned high schools in the area] . . . even though I wanted to go to [name of zoned high school] because there was fashion and stuff and then all my friends [are applying there] . . . I started just looking over the book by myself and then my sisters were like, "Let me see what you picked." And when they saw [the local zoned school], they didn't like it.

Thus, for children of Latin American immigrants, the absence of *directive* or *instrumental parent involvement* resulted in three pathways. Some students, particularly second-generation U.S.-born students, ultimately negotiated the complex process without formal adult oversight and did not consult family members when completing applications. These students described choosing high schools alone. Another set of students who also lacked concrete forms of parental engagement depended on older siblings or cousins to direct them toward or away from certain high schools with both positive and negative implications. The last group, composed mostly of recent immigrant students, relied almost exclusively on the recommendations of school personnel since parents and other family members played no part in the process.

FROM HIGH SCHOOL SEARCH TO HIGH SCHOOL ASSIGNMENTS

Three features differentiated the gifted and talented-track students' engagement in the high school choice process from the rest of the eighth-graders at IS 725. First, they used a variety of strategies to research diverse school options and searched for detailed information about specific schools' academic outcomes and offerings. Next, they sought personalized guidance from school personnel and received direction from family members about which schools to consider and ultimately to select. Finally, they focused almost exclusively on schools' academic performance indicators and reputation as reasons for inclusion on their applications. This *strategic* approach to choice resulted from their own efforts to actively pursue additional information and guidance from a range of school, city-wide, and home-based sources and from their greater financial resources and family involvement to start with. Ultimately, students in the gifted and talented track were able to leverage those tools and supports to identify, apply, and gain admission to the most competitive, highest performing high schools in New York City at a much higher rate than their high performing Latino peers with similar eligibility. (Table 1 compares the high school

TABLE 1

High school matching results by academic track

	High Performing High School (N=114)	Middle Performing High School (N=254)	Low Performing High School (N=343)	International High School (N=39)	Supplementary Round (N=108)
Track					
Regular (n=384)	14.3	36.2	49.5	0.0	13.3
ESL (n=109)	7.3	40.4	48.6	3.7	13.8
Bilingual (n=131)	7.6	19.9	45.8	26.7	17.6
SPED (n=42)	16.7	35.7	47.6	0.0	23.8
Honors (n=58)	20.7	48.3	31.0	0.0	10.3
Gifted and Talented (n=26)	84.6	7.7	7.7	0.0	7.7
TOTAL (n=750)	15.2	33.9	45.7	5.2	14.3

assignments for all 750 eighth graders enrolled at IS 725 at the time of my study, disaggregated by academic track.)

Whereas 84.6% of students in the gifted and talented track were assigned to high schools with at least an 80% four-year graduation rate (labeled in the table as "High performing high schools), only 20.7% of students in the honors track received similar assignments. Instead, 48.3% of honors track students were assigned to high schools with four-year graduation rates of between 65% and 80% (labeled in the table as "Middle performing high schools) and another 31% of them were placed in schools with graduation rates below 65% (labeled in the table as "Low performing high schools). Nearly all of the highest performing high schools had minimum grade and test score requirements (including the SHSAT), and students in the gifted and talented track universally met these eligibility thresholds. However, the size of the gap suggests that factors other than academic achievement were in play as well. The cumulative, coordinated supports that gifted and talented track students received from their peers, school personnel, and family members were almost entirely absent in the lives of Latino youth. Rather, there was a lack of cross-pollination among the developmental spheres of the Latino students (high and low performing alike) at IS 725. Their disjointed, inconsistent, and generally solitary high school choice experiences resulted in assignments to lower performing high schools on average.

The story is even bleaker for the average and low performing students at IS 725 in the regular track, self-contained special education classes, the ESL program, and the bilingual classes. Students' high school assignments are, in effect, the product of their previous academic performance (affecting eligibility for high performing screened schools) and their own school selections. Due to low grades and test scores, many of these students were effectively barred from most of the high schools with high graduation rates. Nearly half of regular-track students (49.5%) were matched to high schools with four-year graduation rates below 65% as were the majority of ESL (48.6%), special education (47.6%), and bilingual (45.8%) track students. These outcomes are consistent with the results of a recent large-scale analysis of high school assignments in New York City between 2007 and 2011. It showed that low-achieving students were matched to high schools that performed worse, on average, in terms of graduation rates, attendance, and *Progress Report* grades than higher achieving peers.[11]

Recent immigrant students' applications tended to be virtually identical, including only the international high schools and/ or the large zoned high schools in their neighborhoods that had bilingual education programs. While only 7.3% and 7.6% of ESL and bilingual-track students, respectively, were matched to high schools with graduate rates above 80%, over a quarter of bilingual track students (26.7%) were assigned to international high schools—high schools specifically designed to meet the needs of recent immigrant students with average six-year graduation rates between 70 and 90 percent. The concentration of recent immigrant students in the international high schools provides some indication that school personnel involvement in any capacity, even without personalized counseling and guidance, may help students narrow the field to focus on more appropriate options.

The percentage of students in each academic track that did not receive a match in the first round is also revealing. Special education students were the most likely to have been deferred to the supplementary round (23.8%) followed by bilingual (17.6%), ESL (13.8%), and regular-track (13.3%) students. The school-wide total of 14.3% of students deferred to the supplementary round far exceeded the districtwide figure reported from the previous year, when 8.8% of students did not receive a first round match.[12] Only half of schools from the first round had seats available in the supplementary round, and few of the high performing schools were still accepting students. Consequently, over 65% of students from IS 725 who participated in the supplementary round were eventually assigned to low performing high schools with graduation rates below 65%.

The majority of eighth-grade students at IS 725 demonstrated a generally consistent pattern of confusion about and minimal investment in the high school choice process. Recent immigrant students in particular knew few details about the different schools or about how the process worked overall. Milton's experience learning about his high school match provides a poignant illustration of recent immigrant students' weak comprehension of the choice process. This, together with the low-income Latino honors-track students' disproportionately low rates of admission to high performing high schools relative to the Asian-origin gifted and talented-track students provides evidence of the weak validity of equity claims about high school choice.

Unexpected legal battles around school closures delayed NYCDOE from releasing high school assignment letters in spring 2010. As a result, rather than distributing the letters to students at school as was customary in past years, the letters were mailed to students' homes over spring break. Many recent immigrant students did not know to expect these letters at home or had forgotten that they would even be receiving their high school assignments. More than two weeks after the letters had been sent in the mail, at least ten recent immigrant students did not know which high school they would be attending in the fall. Finally, Milton found his letter. He had moved in the middle of the school year, and it had been sent to his former mailing address. Even after receiving the letter, though, Milton still did not know his high school assignment. Milton explained: "I read a letter, a letter arrived for me but I also got a new thing [application] to fill out. It didn't say which high school I am going to" [translated from Spanish by the author].

In fact, Milton had not been assigned to any high school. Instead, he had received a blank application for the supplementary round. Because he found out so late about his failure to be matched in the first round, he had less than a week to review the remaining high schools and complete his application form again. He was not alone in this situation. However, no adult, either at the school level or at home, was monitoring his results. Whereas the gifted and talented-track students described running home after school to check for their "match letters," many recent immigrant students were completely unaware of their expected delivery. Dejected and without guidance, Milton ended up putting the same local zoned high school on his supplementary-round application he described as wanting to avoid earlier in the year.

These high school choice experiences and outcomes put into sharp relief the impact of differential access to supports and resources on student engagement in school choice, school selection, and high school assignments. At the same time, the gifted and talented track students' success sheds light on possible interventions that might better equip all students to access high-quality educational opportunities. The next chapter more fully develops the *strategic choice* framework, including the concepts of an *institutional compass* and a *multiply reinforced orientation*. The structural and institutional arrangements and familial practices that contributed to gifted and talented-track students' effectiveness in strategically engaging in high school choice are also examined.

——— ∎∎∎ ———

CHAPTER FIVE

Strategic Versus Passive Approaches

School Choice as a Developmental Opportunity

DESPITE BEING COMPARABLE candidates for admission to academically competitive high schools, higher income Asian students in the magnet gifted and talented program at IS 725 were significantly more likely than the children of lower income Latin American immigrants to be assigned to the most selective, highest performing high schools. Although a number of factors contribute to students' ultimate high school placements in New York City, including their own ordered preferences, the gifted and talented-track students benefited from receiving consistent messages from peers, school personnel, and highly involved family members about how to properly search for high schools and which schools merited consideration. Similar guidance, involvement, and recurrent messages were missing from the lower income Latino students' choice experiences.

The obstacles to achieving an equitable distribution of educational opportunities by way of high school choice do not end there. The undersupply of academically rigorous high schools in

New York City relegates a large majority of students—particularly the lowest achieving students and those with special needs—to high schools with alarmingly poor academic outcomes. City-wide and national data on educational achievement and life-course outcomes associated with school quality point to some potential consequences of students' uneven access to high-quality schooling in New York City. To start, students attending more selective high schools in New York City are more likely to graduate and more likely to meet the state's college readiness standards.[1] Preparedness for postsecondary education has never been more important in light of recent economic transformations, the earnings premium for college-degree holders, and growing evidence of stagnant college completion rates despite skyrocketing enrollment.[2]

As important, the high school choice process in New York City represents considerably more than just a means for students and families to select high schools. In an ideal situation, school choice also provides students and families an opportunity to develop important, transferrable skills that extend far beyond the immediate realm of high school choice (in New York City and elsewhere). They can learn how to access information about public services like schools, identify and analyze metrics of quality, evaluate a range of options, generate a system of prioritization or schema for ordering preferences, and develop strategies to improve their chances of earning a competitive placement—in a school, university, or workplace.

The gifted and talented-track students' *strategic choice* behaviors exemplify the skills and strategies that can be employed to successfully participate in and benefit from bureaucratic processes like high school choice. These students had a precise, almost automated, approach to finding their way through the high school choice labyrinth, what I have been calling an *institutional compass*. Additionally, their school choices were strictly guided by a clear set of criteria or a *multiply reinforced orientation* that narrowed their school search to only those that met certain academic standards. Together, the institutional compass and the multiply reinforced orientation helped them strategically negotiate the process and gain admission to the city's best high schools. In this chapter, the key components of strategic choice—an institutional compass and multiply reinforced orientation—will be defined and explored. It examines the structural and institutional arrangements and familial practices that contributed to gifted and talented-track students' effectiveness in strategically engaging in high school choice and considers the roles of districts and schools in promoting strategic choice behaviors and the associated skills among all students.

DEFINING AN INSTITUTIONAL COMPASS AND A MULTIPLY REINFORCED ORIENTATION

An *institutional compass* is essentially a coherent plan, approach, or navigation tool—akin to a car's global positioning system (GPS)—that people can use to decipher and negotiate bureaucracies, institutional relationships, or other complex policies and processes, including school choice. The institutional compass that proved valuable for successful participation in high school choice in New York City comprised three core elements: (1) an understanding of the details of the choice policy, the school system as a whole, and how to access information about schools; (2) knowledge of the key school-level performance metrics and indicators of academic quality available to consumers; and (3) access to family supports that matched the New York City Department of Education's expectations. In other words, it required actively involved parents who researched schools, formed opinions, and guided and advised their children on school selections.

The concept of an institutional compass is rooted, in part, in Pierre Bourdieu's notion of cultural capital.[3] Defined as resources, knowledge, skills, and experiences that confer privileges on people who possess them, generations of scholars in the field of education and beyond have drawn on this concept to understand and explicate how social and economic advantages get perpetuated in societies and through institutions like schools.[4] Knowledge of how to best take advantage of educational policies is a valuable form of cultural capital. This book shows how certain students and parents effectively activated this form of cultural capital to their benefit in the context of choosing high schools in New York City through the use of an institutional compass. The equity premise of the choice policy is questioned in light of students' differential access to an institutional compass based on parental education, income, and nativity.

While an institutional compass proved to be a vital part of strategic choosers' toolkits, it did not operate in isolation. Students (and parents) who exhibited strategic choice behaviors also had a defined set of principles for choosing schools that was informed and influenced by various people in their social worlds. In other words, they developed a multiply reinforced orientation to certain (typically high performing) high schools. This multiply reinforced orientation usually resulted in their eliminating high schools that did not meet a minimum threshold of academic performance or selectivity (based on high school graduation rates, college enrollment data, and admissions requirements). It provided clarity of focus that helped choosers limit their school searches and ignore most of the seven hundred options that did not meet the standard. Strategic choosers thus employed their institutional compass in pursuit of the goal of obtaining admission to one of a select number of high performing high schools that were deemed acceptable by individuals within their overlapping ecological spheres (in Uri Brofenbrenner's definition of the term).[5] By contrast, passive choosers possessed little, if any, of the pertinent and expected knowledge and cultural capital and lacked a similarly well-developed choice philosophy or goals.

The alignment of several social and developmental milieus and recurring, identical instructions were essential aspects of the strategic choosers' relative success in navigating high school choice in New York City. The uniformity in the messages strategic choosers received from peers, school personnel, and family members about appropriate school search methods and choices had a multiplicative power in terms of guiding their behaviors. It also contributed to their formation of an institutional compass and a multiply reinforced orientation. The extreme degree of integration among peer-, home-, and school-based supports that characterized gifted and talented students' high school choice experiences epitomizes the conditions needed for the development of these tools. Conversely, the low-income Latino students' disjointed developmental contexts, unfocused approaches, and solitary choice-making reflected a lack of institutional compass and a diffuse orientation, which were associated with passive choice behaviors. Understanding how the integration of home and school messages and supports actually works, contributes to skill development, and can be achieved is a first step in helping all students and families develop some form of institutional compass and multiply reinforced orientation that may prove useful in a range of personal, professional, and educational contexts.

Integrated Developmental and Social Spheres

Cultural, socioeconomic, and nativity factors alone cannot adequately explain differences in students' school choice behaviors and experiences—in their possession and use of an institutional compass, their development of a clear set of choice criteria (multiply reinforced orientation), and in their varying degrees of success in obtaining high performing high school placements. The gifted and talented track students' access to each of these tools depended on the existence, transmission, and enactment of certain values and beliefs associated with effective school search strategies. The prominent roles that parents, siblings, and other relatives played in the gifted and talented students' school choice experiences reflected an aspect of their families' habitus, or deeply embedded beliefs, values, and dispositions, that corresponded with the New York City Department of Education's normative assumptions of parental involvement.[6] This correspondence of beliefs and behaviors proved to be a critical component of the students' institutional compass. Next, the weight given to high schools' academic characteristics in the formation of their multiply reinforced orientation encouraged the gifted and talented-track students to focus on activities that would improve their chances of being assigned to an academically rigorous, high performing high school. This was at least in part a product of parents' emphasis on these school qualities.

Favorable effects associated with shared behavioral standards has been well documented by researchers in a number of fields. One of the best-known studies of neighborhood and violent crime rates in Chicago showed a positive association between strong, supportive relationships among neighbors and lower crime rates.[7] Sociologists Robert Sampson, Stephen Raudenbush, and their colleague Felton Earls argued that well-aligned neighborhood structures, values, and processes produced a *collective efficacy* that resulted from positive social control. This process of collective efficacy resulting from reinforced norms was parallel in many ways to the positive impact on gifted and talented students' choices of consistently communicated ideas from peers, school personnel, and family members. In the end, the fusion of home- and school-level supports created a protective and nurturing cocoon that guided gifted and talented students in their exploration and pursuit of high schools that were best suited to their interests and would help them achieve academic and professional goals.

Social Closure in the Development of a Multiply Reinforced Orientation

Powerful messages about acceptable school choices informed the multiply reinforced orientation that nearly every student in the gifted and talented track adopted. Yet in addition to repeated messages, specific structures were needed to transform norms into a more solidified orientation. In this case, a cohesive classroom unit created the conditions for social closure to occur, which facilitated the recurrent transmission and enforcement of messages and norms about appropriate behaviors and goals.

In his definitive piece on the subject of social capital, sociologist James Coleman describes in detail how social closure, or a closed social system, lays the foundation for collective norms, sanctions, and rewards.[8] He applied the idea of social closure directly to school settings and contrasted cases of lower and higher degrees of closure, the latter reflecting situations in which peers "see each other daily, have expectations toward each other, and develop norms about each other's behavior."[9] Students in the gifted and talented class all subscribed to the same set of beliefs about what constituted a good high school. Perhaps more importantly, they shared a firm notion of which schools were unacceptable. The structure of their schooling—specifically, the fact that they had been together since sixth grade, traveled as a class from period to period, and had limited contact with students from other classes or tracks—created conditions in which social closure and, by extension, the exchange of social capital could naturally occur.

The social closure stemming from gifted and talented students' tightly knit, highly regulated classroom community enabled the reinforcement of norms. These norms served as the glue that melded home and school-based elements into their particular orientation toward only academically rigorous, elite high schools. By contrast, references to social closure and concomitant norms were entirely absent in the narratives of high-achieving Latino honors students. A well-integrated network of supports can help students appreciate and internalize the significance of high school choice and ultimately understand how to make academically beneficial choices. On the other hand, uncoordinated or sporadic messages and guidance may prevent students from fully taking advantage of choice options. Although many of the high performing, lower income Latino students shared their gifted and talented peers' ideas about what constituted a desirable high school, these ideas did not exist within a complete or consistent strategy. Nor were they sufficient to translate into necessarily beneficial actions, choices, and outcomes.

MISSED OPPORTUNITIES AND CONSEQUENCES OF CURRENT POLICY

Linking High School and College Choice

Many gifted and talented students expressed considerable anxiety about the task of choosing high schools. At the same time, they described engaging in an exciting and rigorous developmental exercise. It helped them learn or sharpen a range of widely applicable research, analytical, and social skills. By virtue of being embedded in a nurturing social web, school choice actually served as an opportunity for them to grow and expand their knowledge, self-advocacy skills, and experience playing the role of consumer. Other students' accounts of passive choice in no way resembled the high-intensity, stimulating, and well-organized process related by their gifted and talented-track peers. Some of them found it dull; others found it interesting or enjoyable, but uniformly, applying to high school was something they did quickly, with minimal stress and time investment, and generally alone. Consequently, it failed to serve the same capacity-building or developmental function for them.

There are numerous parallels between the process of searching for and applying to high school in New York City and college choice in the United States. The high school choice policy therefore offers a valuable training ground for students to begin to hone the skills necessary to effectively identify appropriate schools, evaluate options, and make important educational decisions as early as middle school. The gifted and talented students recognized the strong similarities between choosing high schools in New York City and choosing colleges, and they used this experience as a practice round for the college search. Krista, a student in the gifted and talented track, explained: "In New York City, I like that you have these different choices so this seems like college, a mini-college process, and you get to choose all these schools." They also understood their high school placements to be directly related to their eventual chances for admission to competitive colleges and universities. For example, Monisha explained the appeal of Specialized High School A in terms of its renowned preparation for college:

> [I put] Specialized High School A because of [its] rigorous curriculum and they offer a lot of college credits, and I've heard that most people who go to college after that came back and said that Specialized High School A was much harder than college. And I thought that it would be good to prepare myself for college, and my mom wanted me to go there too.

The resemblance of New York City's high school choice process to applying to college came up in nearly every interview with gifted and talented students. By contrast, not one student in any of the other academic tracks mentioned it. Development of the transferrable skills and tools necessary for strategic choice (such as an institutional compass) could be particularly beneficial for lower income immigrant and minority students' college access. Research has shown that these youth tend to enroll in less academically selective colleges and universities than they are qualified to attend at higher rates than higher income and white and Asian students.[10] They also have lower college completion rates despite increased participation in postsecondary education in recent years.[11] Early college awareness and strategic search skills (including an institutional compass and a multiply reinforced orientation) may help counteract patterns contributing to stagnant social mobility. These forms of knowledge and techniques can contribute to more informed and engaged decision making in the context of educational choices and can also be used to negotiate a range of institutional and social settings beyond the education system over the course of a person's lifetime.

The Transferability of Strategic Choice Skills

The transferability of a context-specific institutional compass and its manifold benefits vis-à-vis engagement with formal institutions is similar to the health-related advantages that anthropologists Robert Levine, Sarah Levine, and Beatrice Schnell found associated with greater maternal literacy and additional years of schooling for girls in Nepal, Mexico, Venezuela, and Zambia.[12] They identified better educated girls' familiarity with the "academic register" or "the official language of all bureaucracies including health and family-planning clinics as well as schools" as a critical factor in their relatively superior outcomes in reproductive health, child-rearing, and overall health behaviors:

> In schools girls . . . acquire a set of communication skills that they would be unlikely to learn in other settings . . . We propose that the academic register, with its feature of formality, impersonality, and abstractness, is the official language of all bureaucracies . . . Thus, women who spent more time in school know *in advance* much of the language used in public health in clinic settings—not the technical vocabulary but the use of general terms, forms of interrogation, and forms of explanation. This knowledge enables the mothers to learn from professional verbal communication . . . In their world, academic language proficiency and other communication skills acquired in school are the passports to maternal and child health.[13]

Like the academic register, an institutional compass is composed of multiple parts, including accurate information (about a policy, procedures, or opportunities), behaviors that conform to expectations and assigned responsibilities (explicit or not), and knowledge about how to manufacture advantage within a situation of institutional constraints (e.g., scarcity of high-quality educational options). This last element represents a form of cultural capital that must be activated to produce benefits. Just as cultural capital may be simultaneously unique to particular situations (e.g., using school choice to secure a high-quality school placement) and applicable to a broader set of circumstances, the institutional compass needed for effective navigation of high school choice in New York City is both context-specific and includes general skills and knowledge.

The Role of Schools in Developing Strategic Choice Skills

The dramatic variability in students' cultural capital and use of strategic choice tools provides clear indication that all families are not equally equipped to comprehend and successfully negotiate education policies like high school choice in New York City. By taking for granted that all students possess or will have access to adequate supports and guidance to thoughtfully identify appropriate schools, NYCDOE set the stage for this choice process to reproduce rather than counteract historical patterns of educational inequality based on class, race, immigrant origin, and cultural/ethnic background. At the school level, the failure to establish formal structures for counseling about high schools and building knowledge and skills to determine which schools are suitable options and how to gain admission to them was a valuable opportunity squandered. All students at this developmental stage stand to gain from such guidance. Children of low-income immigrants with limited exposure to American educational policies, practices, and expectations might benefit in particular, given the uniquely important role that schools have been shown to play in the lives of recent immigrant students and their families as information disseminators, cultural translators, and socializing bodies.[14]

Schools are well positioned to provide students (and their families) relevant information, help them generate valuable cultural capital, and create conditions for their development of a multipurpose institutional compass. This can occur through direct instruction, supported simulation activities, and structural changes that foster norms, skills, and strategies. Numerous studies have already shown that low-income and minority families depend more on school-based sources of information and advice about educational decisions than white parents and those with higher education levels.[15] Although schools alone may be unable to furnish sufficient guidance to position low-income students on equal footing with their more affluent peers when competing for access to a scare supply of high performing schools, these students are undoubtedly worse off without any institutional support at all.

Institutional Exclusion and Alienation

Sociologist Ricardo Stanton-Salazar warned about *institutional exclusion* as a consequence of "low-status" students not receiving explicit school-based instruction and exposure to skills, resources, and expertise that could facilitate future academic or professional advancement (i.e., an institutional compass). His conclusions, drawn from research with Mexican American and immigrant youth in California secondary schools, apply to the case of Latino, immigrant-origin youth and high school choice in New York City as well:

> Interactions with significant others and agents are usually plentiful, often *caring* (even pleasant), although such interactions rarely rise to the level of master-and-apprentice or the dialogic transfer of institutional support, including cultural knowledge funds and critical insight. On the whole, these interactions are not fundamentally organized (or are unable to organize) to ensure that low-status children and adolescents receive the social, emotional, and institutional resources necessary for optimal development and mobility; nor are they organized to ensure that these young people truly master the greater institutional matrix, including overlapping hierarchies and subordinating forces that socially structure it.[16]

Stanton-Salazar also identified increased alienation and student disaffection from school as potential consequences of education systems' failure to adequately engage with and support students. Defining alienation as "a condition of embeddedness in a social web that socially engages but does not nourish, a web that occupies and partially integrates but does not enable the young individual to actualize his or her full human potential," Stanton-Salazar found widespread evidence of this among the student population he studied.[17] The Latin American immigrant-origin and African American students interviewed from IS 725 did not evince signs of alienation per se in response to their high school choice experiences. However, by being denied explicit school-based guidance and direction, an exclusionary process that may eventually lead to alienation was set in motion. Requiring students to actively seek out recommendations and advice about choosing high schools rather than establishing automatic or mandatory meetings and discussions at the school level placed an excessive burden on them. Stanton-Salazar would associate this negligence on the part of schools with social reproduction and potentially serious individual-level developmental repercussions for students:

> In the final analysis, differential conditions and opportunities for learning to mobilize institutional support effectively may represent another key dimension of the school's *hidden curriculum* . . . Negative embeddedness, especially an aversion to help seeking during adolescence, might not only spell future social death in key adult institutional arenas (e.g., the labor market) but could also position low-status individuals to experience the worst possible side effects of class and racial forces . . . Institutional exclusion works through the processes that tacitly function to get the excluded and dispossessed to regulate and reinforce their own marginality. It also permits us to "blame the victim."[18]

For eighth-grade students charged with applying to high school in New York City, the institutional exclusion that Stanton-Salazar cited could take multiple forms and transcend issues of high school placement alone. In the most concrete terms, students can be blocked from admission to the highest performing high schools for a variety of reasons: their own poor performance in seventh grade may make them ineligible for entry into competitive screened schools; limited exposure to material covered on the specialized high school admissions test in school and minimal preparation for the exam outside of school may result in lower scores and reduced likelihood of admission. Weak guidance from school personnel, family members, or other people in their social networks may also restrict the range of options they explore and/or pursue. Students who are dissatisfied with their high school assignments may become disillusioned, feel cheated by the high school choice process and the education system more generally, and could enter high school with limited faith in their academic chances or motivation to succeed at this important juncture in their educational careers.

In sum, if schools do not provide such information to students and families about high school choice and assist students in making appropriate and realistic selections—in part by helping them develop an institutional compass of their own—the probability of high school choice advancing educational equity is significantly reduced. Rather, under the banner of freedom of choice, long-standing cycles of disadvantage and privilege are poised to continue uninterrupted. The conclusion describes some of the kinds of activities, programs, and structures that schools, family members, and community-based organizations could use to help counteract these unequal and exclusionary processes. Many of them focus on how to help all students begin to generate the strategic choice skills and sensibilities that will better position them for success in competitive school choice, college, and professional marketplaces.

FROM STUDENTS TO PARENTS

Students are at the heart of this book about the challenges to achieving equity through high school choice in New York City. Yet students' experiences can tell only part of the story. Parents take center stage in the next chapter. It focuses on their understandings of and ideas about high school choice in New York City and their varying forms of participation in the choice process. High-income white parents' and low-income Latin American immigrant parents' different philosophies of child-rearing, anxieties about their children's futures, and resources contributed to choice behaviors ranging from strategic to passive. The chapter discusses the roots of these differences and their implications for achieving equity through school choice in New York City.

———— ■■■ ————

CHAPTER SIX

Parents' Roles, Students' Responsibilities

Cultural Values and the Premises of School Choice

IN THEORY, HIGH school choice in New York City brings together three separate actors—school personnel, students, and parents—in pursuit of a common goal: a desirable, appropriate high school placement. The idea of choice as a collaborative endeavor among these actors is at the core of the New York City Department of Education's theory of high school choice and informs its expectations of schools, students, and parents in the process. To this point, the book has focused on students and school personnel and has shown the disconnect between NYCDOE's assumptions and expectations and their actual school choice behaviors and experiences. This chapter completes the picture by examining parents' perspectives on and participation in high school choice.

Earlier chapters identified variation in parental involvement as one contributing factor to students' propensity to engage in *strategic* versus *passive* choice. Yet the choice narratives were told entirely from students' points of view. Here, parents' understandings, beliefs, goals, and actual activities vis-à-vis high school choice are presented in their own words. Interviews with low-income Latin American immigrant parents and higher income native-born white parents of eighth-grade students in New York City show parents' vastly different views on and degrees of participation in high school choice by income, education, and nativity.[1] The correspondence between NYCDOE's expectations and upper-middle-class white parents' approaches to choice is consistent with the well-documented alignment between education policies and white, middle-class norms.[2] Conversely, the low-income Latin American immigrant parents' views and behaviors, which depart significantly from expectations, raise questions about the basic assumptions driving many school choice policies like New York City's.

PARENTAL ENGAGEMENT IN CHOICE AND SCHOOLING

Parents of eighth-grade students faced with a mandatory high school choice policy in New York City approached and experienced it in noticeably different ways. They showed substantial variation in their comprehension of the policy, in their level of involvement in choosing high schools, in their ideas and information about schools in New York City, and, perhaps most significantly, in their estimation of the importance of their child's final high school assignment. Whereas the low-income Latin American immigrant parents exemplified *passive choice*, higher income native-born white parents provided extreme examples of *strategic choice* behaviors. Yet language barriers, background knowledge about New York City schools, and unequal resources only partially explain parents' engagement in passive versus strategic high school choice with (or on behalf of) their eighth-grade children. Instead, the variation observed can also be attributed to parents' ideas about child-rearing, their views on the appropriate division of labor between parents and children, and to possession or lack of an effective institutional compass to negotiate the high school choice maze.

Low-income Latin American immigrant and upper-middle-class white parents' choice behaviors and perspectives diverged in four key areas. First, parents' roles in making high school decisions for and/or with their eighth-grade children were dissimilar. Next, they relied on few of the same sources of information to learn about high schools in New York City. Third, their school selection criteria were vastly different. Last, the reported breakdown of tasks between parents and their eighth-grade children was dissimilar. It ranged from parents spearheading the entire process with minimal child input at one extreme to an entirely child-led approach in which parents' sole responsibility was to sign the completed application form at the other. These differences in the division of labor were in part a reflection of parents' larger ideas about child development and their child-rearing philosophies. They also signaled divergent views of the significance of a high school assignment for a student's educational and life-course outcomes.

Extreme Engagement: Upper-Middle-Class White Parents' High School Choice Behaviors

Upper-middle-class white parents considered the task of finding a high-quality, safe, and academically rigorous high school for their child an exceedingly important life event. It was also one of the most stress-inducing experiences they had undergone as parents. Securing a spot in one of the few high performing high schools in New York City was a monumental endeavor, and the results of the high school choice process had a number of potentially serious implications for these families. Parents discussed their child's high school assignment as possibly impacting the family's financial security and residential decisions, the child's college prospects, and, perhaps most significantly, his/her physical and psychological well-being.

For some families, a child's high school assignment meant the difference between staying in New York City or moving to the suburbs where they could be guaranteed a "good" education; for others, it meant either paying the expensive tuition at a Manhattan private school or saving nearly $40,000 a year on school fees. For the upper-middle-class parents who did not have the flexibility to change residences or could not afford private school tuition, a student's high school "match" signified whether he/she would be educated in a secure and academically challenging environment or whether his/her life would be threatened and academic progress thwarted. For example, Eileen, an experienced school choice participant who had gone through elementary, middle, and high school choice in New York City with three children and the college application process with two, described the choice process in the following way:

> It's worse than applying to college. I've been through that twice . . . If you don't get your first choice of colleges, you are not going to get beat up at your second choice. Your life isn't in danger if instead of going to Wesleyan you go to SUNY-Albany. It's not the same with high schools. There are some really bad ones out there . . . Now in New York City there are some schools in the system that are phenomenal. Some of the best in the country. But there are also a lot of schools in the system where the child is in danger, their life is in danger. The stakes are really high . . . Right now there are, maybe, 20 percent of schools are really good, 5 percent are fabulous. Then there are tons of terrible schools—just really bad. The teachers are tired of teaching, that's the real problem. And there just aren't enough good schools available.

Upper-middle-class white parents invested a tremendous amount of time, financial resources, and emotional and psychological energy in the task of identifying, visiting, reviewing, and choosing suitable high schools for and with their children. Parents reported attending anywhere from ten to twenty-five open houses, spending thousands of dollars on specialized test preparation services and tutoring, hiring private education consultants, and taking multiple days off from work to search for schools, organize materials, and participate in events. They purchased books about New York City high schools; sought advice from friends, colleagues, other parents, and middle school personnel; and spent hours combing the Internet for relevant information. Kathy, the mother of high-achieving twin girls who was navigating high school choice for the first time, articulated a clear plan of action:

> I did a lot of work on this. I checked out when the high school tours were; the website for the DOE; the website from [her daughters' middle school]; and the blog that the parent coordinator wrote for [middle school] eighth-grade classes. Both of our girls took in-house tutorials at [middle school] for the specialized high school tests. We sent them off to summer camp with test prep books. They rode horses and did test prep. We signed both our girls up for GRF [Test Preparation], which tutors kids for the specialized high school exams . . . We talked to other parents who had older children to get an idea of where kids applied . . . I was addicted to insideschools.org [a website with descriptions and reviews of schools in New York City].

Repeatedly, these parents described high school choice as the most harrowing educational experience of their lives. According to Kathy, "I felt like it was almost another full-time job. There was a lot of stress . . . We pretty much determined that we would move [if they did not like the results] so I was also looking at school districts and houses in Long Island . . . While the high school process puts a lot of stress on the parents, I think that the stress that it puts on the kids is unconscionable. There has to be a better way than this." Eileen had actual physical manifestations of anxiety associated with high school choice: "With my oldest, when she finally found out about her high school, I realized I'd been grinding my teeth; I had so much tension in my neck."

School academic outcomes reign supreme

The sample of upper-middle-class white parents universally believed that school quality varied greatly across New York City. Much like the students in the gifted and talented track at IS 725,

they also shared a common understanding of what constituted satisfactory school characteristics; consequently, they relied on a fixed,
narrow set of criteria for determining which schools were worth
considering. These criteria, in turn, guided the parents' search for
information about schools for their children.

Upper-middle-class white parents repeatedly mentioned that
there were only nine or ten "good" high schools in the entire city
to which they were willing to send their children. Some parents
limited their children to only six or seven schools. They evaluated
schools based on admissions requirements (grades and test scores)
and the competitiveness of admission, SAT and Regents scores,
college acceptances, and reputation or what they had heard directly from other trusted sources. Kathy's discussion of the way
in which she and her husband determined which schools were
acceptable was representative of nearly every upper-middle-class
parent's account:

> Our girls both had 90+ averages and good State test scores. If they did
> not get into a specialized high school, we wanted them to go to a good
> screened school. We preferred a good school in the neighborhood or
> at least Manhattan, and there are a limited number of choices . . . If I
> didn't like the colleges they [the high school's graduates] got into, we
> wouldn't put it. We [she and her husband] grew up on Long Island, in
> Levittown. There were not great schools. That affected our colleges,
> so I wanted our daughters to have more options.

Other parents talked about the challenges they encountered
when attempting to access certain school performance data. Martha, the mother of an eighth-grade boy who was going through
the choice process for the first time, complained, "It was really a
year of an incredible amount of effort. An incredible amount of
research. But it was hard finding some information . . . I wanted to
find out SAT scores and it was really hard. A lot of schools that got
A ratings [on NYCDOE *Progress Reports*] had low SAT scores." In
addition to demonstrating their level of investment in identifying

suitable high schools, such comments reflect these parents' deeper knowledge of the range of academic metrics that exist and could be used to evaluate school quality.

For affluent parents of lower performing students, the process of identifying schools was even more difficult and anxiety-provoking because their children often did not qualify for the most competitive, best-known schools in the city. Therefore, they had to expand their search beyond the traditional, limited range of schools and explore lesser known alternatives. While most parents expressed strong concerns about safety regardless of their child's academic performance, it was a particularly prominent theme in interviews with upper-middle-class white parents of lower performing students; they relayed a palpable sense of fear that their children would be endangered academically or physically if they did not get accepted into a "good" school. For example, Eileen discussed her son's situation as follows:

> My son is a smart boy with learning issues. It was clear to him and us that he wasn't going to go to Stuyvesant or one of the exam schools, so he didn't take the Stuyvesant test. It would have been a bad fit . . . I went through the book, looked for schools with collaborative team teaching (CTT) and that were academically rigorous so that eliminated a lot . . . There were some that had 50 percent graduation rates and CTT but were not good. Schools with high graduation rates and CTT were harder to find, but my son is a bright kid . . . We went to look at some of the schools. The tours were extremely instructive. One school was sweet and lovely but for stupid kids. My child would die there. So that was out. At another school the person from the school staff doing the introduction was a total dummy. We ran away in the middle of the tour. It was just totally unbelievable.

Ultimately, Eileen and other parents in similar situations relied heavily on personal recommendations from other parents who were familiar with lesser known schools that would still meet their minimum academic and safety criteria. In fact, word-of-mouth proved to be crucial for all upper-middle-class white parents. Like their common school selection criteria, these parents reported relying on a nearly identical list of information sources.

Standardized information sources

More than once, parent interviewees responded to a standard interview question about the steps they took to learn about schools by explaining that they did "what everyone does." This included purchasing the same book about the best public high schools in New York City, attending open houses and fairs, perusing the NYCDOE website, reading reviews on InsideSchools.org, and speaking to a large number of friends, family members, colleagues, and school personnel.[3] Without fail, these parents named members of their social network, which included parents of their children's friends, members of the school PTA, friends, work colleagues, and academic tutors as the most important sources of information about how to successfully negotiate the choice process and which schools to consider. One mother described her most valuable information source as the "mom gossip network," explaining: "The other really strong thing is the mom gossip network. It is incredibly important, the most important thing . . . None of what you really need is written down so you have to chat people up, parents with older kids, find out what they did. You ask questions—other parents, teachers in school, people who work in the system. That's where you get your best information."

Middle school personnel were named with varying frequency as sources of guidance and information regarding high schools. At one middle school, the PTA raised funds specifically to cover the salary of a dedicated high school articulation counselor. She was described as being intimately involved in almost every aspect of students' and parents' search and decision-making process, and her responsibilities ranged from giving explicit instructions about the number of schools to put down to intervening and lobbying high schools and NYCDOE directly if a student did not receive a satisfactory placement. Parent respondents with children at the two other Manhattan middle schools reported less extensive school engagement such as email updates sent out by guidance counselors and parent coordinators about open houses, deadlines, and events as well as one-on-one meetings and personalized recommendations shared with the child, the parent, or both. These parents made clear their views of school as a supplementary, not primary, source of support and information and one of varying usefulness.

Mary, a first-time participant in high school choice, had high praise for her daughter's guidance counselor: "The [middle school] guidance counselor did a fabulous job keeping us informed. Any scrap of information they get, they share it, they blast it out over email." On the other hand, Joseph, whose son was an eighth-grader at a different middle school, had a less positive view of the role of the middle school personnel: "They had a large session of all parents in the auditorium. They gave us some good information given the format, but . . . there is no individual attention." Even with minor differences in interactions with school personnel and in their information sources, upper-middle-class respondents depicted a relatively uniform scenario in which adults were chiefly responsible for setting up and paying for specialized test preparation and tutoring services, researching different high schools, scheduling school visits, reviewing required essays, and consulting with external advisors. Their children's participation took the form of preparing for the specialized test, accompanying parents to open houses, and voicing final opinions.

A joint parent-child endeavor

After winnowing the number of potential high school candidates to a few acceptable options, parents would present the approved list to their eighth-grade children to solicit feedback and discuss their opinions, either before or after visiting schools. The child's main role was to indicate their school preferences and provide direction to parents in terms of the order in which to rank them on the application. Parents thus completed a significant amount of work up front in an effort to set the stage for their children to make what they considered sound high school decisions. When asked whether the high school choice process was primarily parent- or child-led, nearly all of the upper-middle-class parents responded that it was a joint endeavor. This response was belied by their extensive descriptions of the time and energy they invested in researching schools in comparison to their children's minimal involvement. However, because most of them left the final decisions up to their children—something a number of them explained as being a significant developmental milestone—they understood the process to be a collaborative, shared experience. In fact, many upper-middle-class white parents' conception of their responsibilities in the high school choice process was directly linked to their larger philosophies of child-rearing. As one father explained:

> It was pretty equal in the sense that I made it clear to them that this was going to be their choice; but I also made it clear that I was going to tell them what I thought. I probably would have been more interventionist if I had disagreed with their choices. My theory of child-rearing is that if they are deciding between two very good choices, it's their decision.

Kathy, the mother of the twin girls, also described it as "Kind of a joint process. We [she and her husband] did a lot of work getting information. We stayed on top of fairs, blogs, visits. But when we took them to see fairs, we let them choose; it was up to them to decide which schools they wanted to list." One of her twin daughters confirmed this account and distinguished between her role and that of her parents by explaining, "My parents did a really good job showing me what the choices were." This quote captures the essence of upper-middle-class parents' engagement in the choice process: their primary responsibility was to clear the path so that their children could select among the few high school options they deemed acceptable.

Leaving It Up to the Child: Latin American Immigrant Parents and High School Choice

Latin American immigrant parents fell on the opposite end of the spectrum of engagement in the high school choice process when compared to their higher income, white counterparts. The differences in their approaches to high school choice transcended questions of comprehension of the required procedures or disparities in the amount of time, money, and mental energy invested; philosophical differences existed as well. More specifically, the low-income Latin American parents interviewed did not view oversight of or even participation in their child's high school decisions as part of their parental duties. Additionally, they espoused a relatively universal belief that schools were basically interchangeable and thus their child's ultimate placement was of little consequence as long as he/she was a conscientious student.

Latin American immigrant parents possessed a very basic understanding of how the choice process worked. They also knew very little about the range of high school options available to their children. Parents with older children attending New York City high schools were slightly more familiar with the application and the neighborhood schools than those for whom this was the first child applying; however, even the more experienced parents showed considerable confusion about the details and required procedures. There were also minor differences in parental involvement by country of origin. Parents from the Dominican Republic tended to be the most engaged in high school choice, Mexican parents were the least likely to take on the task of choosing high schools with their children, and Ecuadoran parents fell somewhere in the middle. These country-of-origin differences should be interpreted with caution, however, given the small sample size. Overall, Latin American immigrant parents were minimally, if at all, involved in identifying and deciding which high schools their eighth-grade children should consider.

Limited set of information sources

Unlike upper-middle-class white parents who relied on an extensive range of information sources to learn about educational options in New York City, Latin American immigrant parents cited relatively few. Whereas a number of upper-middle-class parents criticized the high school directory as being too generic and lacking the detailed individual school performance data in which they were most interested, Latin American immigrant parents overwhelmingly named it as the primary and, in many cases, sole source of information that they (or their children) used. Older children, family members, neighbors, and, in a few cases, their children's teachers were also reported as providing information about high schools in New York City. However, in contrast to upper-middle-class white parents who solicited explicit details and personalized advice about specific schools, Latin American immigrant parents described hearing overall opinions and impressions of schools but knew few concrete facts, particularly about a school's academic outcomes.

In the case of Julisa, an eighth-grade student who had come to the United States from the Dominican Republic with her mother less than a year earlier, a stepfather, Antonio, was the primary adult assisting with the high school choice process. A Dominican immigrant himself, Antonio had lived in the U.S. for nearly twenty years and had an older daughter who had been through the process previously. He described his approach to choosing high schools in the following way:

> In reality we did very little. We were guided only by the book that they sent from school, that's in English. The only things we found in there [the directory] were the name of the school, the addresses, to see which was closest. And if we had heard that maybe a school wasn't very good, you see? . . . For example, I have heard that [name of zoned high school] is not very good even though my daughter studied there, you see? Now, I don't really know about that one and other [schools]; I don't have much information. We just . . . put the

ones that were closest and some people also gave us some information. One of her [Julisa's] aunts and teachers also . . . gave their opinions about some schools. They gave them to the girl [Julisa]. We just took a risk. We took a risk by putting down some schools and we'll see what happens. [translated from Spanish by the author]

Minimal expectations of school personnel involvement

Latin American immigrant parents made few references to middle school personnel in their children's high school decisions and expressed minimal expectations of school support and guidance for choice. In fact, only five out of the twenty-four Latin American immigrant parents interviewed cited school-based sources of information, including teachers' recommendations made directly to their child, as influencing their or their children's decisions about which high schools to list on the application. Contrary to findings from earlier educational studies of low-income Latin American immigrant parents, the parents in this study neither assumed nor expected school personnel to provide extensive assistance with the high school choice process.[4] The inconsistency in results may be attributable, in part, to the fact that most studies of low-income Latin American immigrants' involvement in their children's schooling have been conducted with parents of elementary-age students.[5] Yet the findings do constitute a marked departure from the widely held views on Latin American immigrant parents' expectations of school support and responsibilities generally.

Preferred school characteristics

Latin American immigrant parents' expressed school preferences and priorities for their children's high school selections help shed light on this unexpected finding. Most Latin American immigrant interview respondents did not offer unsolicited opinions about specific high schools or ideas about the type of high school they wanted their child to attend. However, when asked directly about what they thought was important, the themes of proximity to home, safety, and attending the same school as siblings or family members were repeated consistently. One Mexican immigrant mother simply stated that "the closer the school is, the better." Marcela and Manuel, Mexican immigrants and parents of Jordan, a high performing second-generation student introduced in chapter 5, were puzzled by his desire to attend a school nearly forty-five minutes away. Despite their older son's difficulty graduating from the local zoned high school—only managing to do so after five years—and his reports of violence there, Marcela and Manuel could not comprehend Jordan's resistance to enrolling in the same school. As Marcela explained:

> I don't know what his problem is with [the zoned high school], why Jordan wants to go to another school farther away. I tell him, "Why do you want to go so far? You are intelligent wherever you go. The cold. If you have to get to school by seven, getting up at five thirty to then take a bus or train at six. I don't like it." [translated from Spanish by the author]

The most striking pattern in Latin American immigrant parents' responses was the pervasive reference made to the belief that "there are no bad schools, only the students inside the schools are bad." Without fail, interview respondents would invoke a variation of this refrain when describing how they felt about the schools in New York City, even after acknowledging the gangs and violence associated with their neighborhood schools. For Marcela, "Any school whether it is pretty or ugly, it doesn't matter. Because for us it doesn't matter if the school is pretty or ugly, it depends on you." Her husband, Manuel, echoed this sentiment: "I don't believe in this that there are bad schools, I don't think there are bad schools . . . Now the people in the school, well, like everything . . . there are good teachers and bad teachers, but in my opinion it is up to the kids."

In the course of discussing their ideas about schools, Latin American immigrant parents put on display their core belief that if their child was a good, hardworking, and respectful student who stayed out of trouble and followed school rules, he/she would succeed in any school context. Consequently, the ultimate school assignment received through the high school choice process was somewhat irrelevant. For example, Antonio rejected claims that certain schools were inherently bad, citing his daughter's and niece's successful academic experiences at one of the supposedly "bad" schools: "A lot of times also it's not just that the school is bad. It's the students who are bad, not really the school. Because my niece went there [zoned high school] and she did not get into trouble. My daughter went there too and she didn't . . . nothing happened either." In essence, this belief in the undifferentiated nature of schools, coupled with low-income Latin American parents' parenting philosophy (described below), helps to further explain their comparatively hands-off approach to the high school choice process and their minimal expectation of school personnel involvement.

Division of labor in relation to child-rearing philosophy

Children in Latin American immigrant families were responsible for conducting any research they deemed necessary about schools and completing the high school application form. Their parents, if involved in any concrete way, generally played a supportive role by commenting on the schools on the list, jointly reviewing the directory with their child, and providing basic encouragement for overall academic achievement. In most cases, parents understood their children to be old enough and mature enough to make sound high school decisions, and they trusted them to do so with minimal oversight. Take Juana, for example, a Mexican immigrant and mother of five whose eldest son, Emilio (introduced in chapter 5), was participating in high school choice for the first time. She explained, "Well, I can't tell him 'You're not going to go to that high school,' because I think, I feel, that if you force them, they aren't going to do it. So, I told him, you pick."

For Manuel, it was a combination of lack of familiarity with the high school options and confidence in Jordan's ability to make sound decisions:

> Well, I have always given him the choice to decide what he wants, no? Always, whatever he thinks, based on what his classmates, what the neighbors say. If they say, "Look, go to this school, it is much better." But my opinion has always been, and I tell him, "No school is better [than any other] if you pay attention. If you pay attention, if you go to what you are supposed to go to, you will always be a good student." I respect his . . . his ideas so he will feel comfortable telling me, "Dad, I don't want to go to school today." If he tells me his reasons why, "Then stay home" [I tell him]. [translated from Spanish by the author]

The Latin American immigrant parents interviewed considered such academic questions as high school selection to fall outside their purview. They focused instead on developing their child's moral character. Throughout the interviews, Latin American immigrant parents clearly distinguished between their responsibilities as parents—which resided almost exclusively in the realm of moral development—and the school-related tasks and decisions that fell to their adolescent children. As such, the relationship between these parents' child-rearing philosophies and their engagement in the high school choice process was elucidated. As Manuel explained:

> He [Jordan] told me about a few schools. The truth is I haven't studied there, I can't tell him, "Excellent," right? What I always tell him is, "Son, whatever you like, it is all a question of doing it with discipline. Get there early, respect your teachers, get to know your teachers. If you don't understand something, you always have to raise your hand and speak with the teacher. The teacher is there to orient you, to help you. Speak up. Ask. Don't stay quiet if you don't know something." . . . Well, I always say, "Son, don't forget, don't forget: dis-

cipline, discipline, discipline. You always have to be alert. From the moment you get on our block, you see people, "How are you, ma'am? Good day." "How are you, sir? Good day." . . . Because the children, we are also educating them." [translated from Spanish by the author]

Reese and her colleagues found evidence of this as well in their study of Mexican immigrant parents. They argued, "Parents see their responsibility as that of giving their children the knowledge necessary for them to follow the 'good path' in life; however, children make the decision for themselves. Eighty-one percent of the ethnographic subset families stated that children make these life-course decisions between the ages of 12 and 18."[6] In sum, rather than attributing these parents' minimal involvement in high school decisions to lack of understanding, language barriers, and limited resources alone, interview data provide a strong case for understanding it in terms of approaches to child development and socialization as well.

CONNECTING HIGH SCHOOL CHOICE AND COLLEGE ACCESS

The disparity in the frequency and nature of parents' references to college proved to be a final dividing line between low-income Latin American immigrant and upper-middle-class white parents' perspectives on high school choice. College acceptances—and, more specifically, the caliber of postsecondary institutions to which a high school's graduates were accepted—proved to be a major concern for upper-middle-class parents. Many of the upper-middle-class parents assiduously pursued this data point, and they understood high school placement as inextricably linked to their child's chances for access to a competitive college. Ultimately, they sought to ensure an unobstructed path of elite schooling from elementary school through postsecondary education. Conversely, the question of college only emerged during interviews with Latin American immigrant parents after prompting or if an older child was attending college, usually a two-year college or training program. When college was discussed, these parents most often shared their anxiety about the costs associated with postsecondary education and expressed a desire for children to pursue the least expensive career tracks. Manuel explained discussions with his eldest son about postsecondary education: "I've always told him that he should try to do a fast degree program and then do more later. It won't cost much that way."

This last distinction in many ways epitomizes the differences in low-income Latin American immigrants' and upper-middle-class white parents' conception of the consequence of high school placement in New York City. Whereas the latter group associated long-term educational and mobility outcomes with high school assignments and experienced considerable anxiety, the former viewed high school choice as little more than another bureaucratic procedure typical of schooling in the United States. They accordingly gave it only perfunctory consideration.

PARENTS AS STRATEGIC AND PASSIVE CHOOSERS

Upper-middle-class white parents exemplified *strategic choice* in its most extreme form. They also expressed a strong, common ideology about what needed to be done to defend, preserve, and ensure their children's safety and educational advancement. This ideology was constantly reinforced by other parents, friends, and colleagues who swept them up in a wave of fear, financial investment, and endless worry.

The almost perfect correlation between upper-middle-class white parents' behaviors and NYCDOE's expectations of parental roles in the high school choice process may only partly explain their success in obtaining high performing high school placements for their children. These parents' narratives very clearly conveyed the fact that their efforts did not occur in isolation. Rather, as was the case for the gifted and talented-track students interviewed at IS 725, upper-middle-class white children lived, learned, and developed in ecological spheres—their home, school, and extracurricular environments—that were highly integrated and focused on the goal of securing satisfactory high school assignments. Beginning in seventh grade when preparations for the specialized high school test began (if not earlier), these students heard virtually identical messages from teachers, guidance counselors, classmates, academic tutors, siblings, friends, and parents about which high schools were acceptable and what it took get admitted to the most competitive ones. The stage was set for the parents' and children's development of a *multiply reinforced orientation* and an *institutional compass* to be used for the purposes of high school choice.

Upper-middle-class white parent interviews provided another near-textbook example of Coleman's theory of social closure at work. In this instance, the family rather than the classroom served as the primary social unit through which the essential standards and expectations were transmitted and emphasized. Therefore, white, upper-middle-class students' high school choice experiences were defined by what Coleman called "intergenerational closure," a situation in which norms are articulated and reinforced by various community institutions.[7] Some scholars have asserted that such intergenerational closure is often more easily achieved in middle-class white families than low-income minority ones because their norms and values are reflected in community policies and institutional practices.[8]

In the end, although high school choice was highly stressful for the white, upper-middle-class parents and their children, the process was also well coordinated and produced favorable results: almost every one of the children of parents interviewed got one of their top three selections. These parents' accounts portrayed an almost hyperbolic version of the gifted and talented students' successful experiences at IS 725 resulting from clear goals (i.e., a multiply reinforced orientation) as well as a blueprint for negotiating the process (i.e., a finely tuned institutional compass). Notably, whereas gifted and talented-track students described taking the helm of their own application process while receiving considerable support from parents and other adults, the upper-middle-class white parents were undoubtedly in the driver's seat despite their assertion of it being a jointly controlled enterprise.

Latin American immigrant parents' *passive choice* behaviors departed considerably from NYCDOE's expressed expectations of parents. Interviews revealed the Latin American immigrant parents to be confident in leaving school selections up to their thirteen- and fourteen-year-old children without the expectation that school personnel would be directing choices or would even be consulted. The ceding of school choice decision-making authority to their children was partially related to the Latin American immigrant parents' espoused belief that all schools were alike. Moreover, these parents repeatedly expressed the opinion that it was the student's responsibility to succeed regardless of the high school he/she attended. That Latin American immigrant parents did not depend on school personnel to advise their children constituted an important, unanticipated finding, offering new insight into their views on adolescent development more generally.[9]

Latin American immigrant parents evinced none of the fear and anxiety that permeated upper-middle-class white parents' narratives. They felt that if they fulfilled their duties of instilling in their child a sense of moral rectitude, a strong work ethic, and a commitment to achievement, their children would be able to choose wisely and succeed in whichever school they ended up being assigned. It is also likely that some parent-child role reversal was in play in many of the Latin American immigrant families, especially when the children were U.S. born.[10] Nonetheless, these data show that the explanations for Latin American immigrant parents' passive engagement in high school choice are entirely more complex than just one factor.

IMPLICATIONS OF VARIATION IN PARENTAL ENGAGEMENT IN HIGH SCHOOL CHOICE

Classification of parent choosers as *strategic* or *passive* builds on what is already known about parents' diverse approaches to choice.[11] It also reveals how middle-class parents use school choice to preserve their children's social status and relative privilege in the education system by identifying some of the strategies and tools that they actually employ.[12] Perhaps most significantly, the side-by-side comparison of high-income, native-born parents' and low-income Latin American immigrant parents' responses to high school choice in the same district challenges one of the underlying premises of school choice theory: the idea that parents' incentives to become informed and involved are automatically and dramatically increased for all participants in a market-based system.[13]

The phenomenon of school systems building a policy on flawed assumptions of parent behavior is not new. In fact, examples of bureaucratic institutions relying on white, middle-class norms in the development of policies geared primarily for low-income and minority populations are plentiful.[14] Yet the well-documented consequences of privileging a particular set of (usually white, middle-class) resources, behaviors, or approaches to child-rearing (e.g., nondominant students' and parents' increased alienation from school, thwarted or delayed academic progress, construction of cultural-deficit ideas among school personnel, perpetuation of social and cultural stratification) are missing a critical lesson learned from the case of high school choice in New York City.[15] Even beyond the issue of obstructing more equitable access to high-quality schools, the faulty theoretical basis and misplaced expectations that undergird school choice policies result in a tremendous lost opportunity for schools to educate and support students and families in a much more comprehensive manner. The previous chapter detailed some of the ways that school choice could be used to help students develop valuable, transferrable skills and knowledge (e.g., in the form of an institutional compass), and these skill-building opportunities could benefit parents as well. The results of this study thus point to additional disadvantages associated with less than expected parental guidance and support in youth's educational experiences and schools' failure to fill in the gap. They also shed light on educational patterns occurring outside the K–12 school choice arena.

High School Choice as College Training Ground

High school choice served as a college-search training ground for many upper-middle-class white families and gifted and talented students at IS 725. Just as the children of upper-middle-class white parents were exposed to the high school application process early on in their middle school years, they also began preparing for the rigors of the competitive college race almost immediately. Their educational experiences were carefully orchestrated to be a single, uninterrupted pathway leading to the final goal of selective college placement. For the gifted and talented-track students as well, the connection between their high school match and college options was clear: they made school selections on the basis of graduates' college placements and competitiveness, and they referenced parallels between New York's choice process and the college search. In essence, the higher income white parents and gifted and talented-track students understood education as a "positional good," or one in which "one's position or relative standing in the distribution of education, rather than one's absolute attainment of education, matters a great deal."[16] This belief directly informed their approach to high school choice.

By contrast, the Latino and African American youth's and their parents' silence on the relationship between high school assignments and access to college reflected a more segmented, short-term perspective on the stages of education. Moreover, there was no indication of their developing applicable skills and college readiness through the high school application process. As such, the documented differences in families' high school choice experiences and perspectives may help to expose and explain the persistent cycles of institutional exclusion that span pre-primary to the collegiate level. The consequences of this are evident in achievement gaps, unequal access to high-quality schools, and disparate college enrollment and completion rates by race/ethnicity and socioeconomic status.[17] Policies directed toward but not aligned with lower income and minority students' diverse norms, philosophies, and practices may actually end up exacerbating rather than counteracting gaps in achievement, creating rather than dismantling barriers to access to educational opportunities or even worsening the very educational inequalities they were supposedly designed to combat.

Legal scholars William J. Koski and Rob Reich warned about this possibility in their discussion of the relationship between education as a "positional good" and the enactment of equity-minded education policies. They argued, "The recent shift away from equity-minded policies to adequacy-minded (equity-neutral) policies must be reconsidered; to the extent that education is a good with strong positional aspects, we need to focus on the comparatively worse off, targeting resources to the needy, and we ought still to object to inequalities even above a threshold of adequacy."[18] In essence, they advocate a return to and expansion of policies that focus explicitly on the needs of disadvantaged populations or "redistributive equity policies" that have been rapidly disappearing in recent years and replaced by "excellence for all" rhetoric and policies.

School choice has been extensively condemned on the grounds that it does just what Koski, Reich, and others have warned against.[19] Critics like Stephen Ball have been particularly vociferous in rejecting the claims of neutrality purported to exist in many school choice policies. Their charge that "Within the education marketplace, this 'mechanism of class transmission' is 'doubly hidden': it is obscured first of all by the continuing assumptions about the neutrality of patterns of achievement in education, and second, by the assumptions about the neutrality of the market itself and by the model and distribution of the 'good parent' upon which it trades," launched nearly two decades ago, still rings true today.[20] Evidence from New York City furthers this and other critiques of choice by upending the basic tenet of school choice theory about parents' attitudes, values, expectations, and behaviors. The final chapter further explicates the notion of a redistributive equity agenda and elaborates a series of policy and programmatic recommendations aimed to leverage the potential of school choice policies to promote equity and transferrable skill development.

CONCLUSION

———■■■———

Policies, Programs, and Activities That Support Strategic Choice

MASS MIGRATION IS changing the face and fabric of societies all over the globe. Schools in immigrant-receiving communities are now educating a more racially, ethnically, culturally, and linguistically diverse student population than ever before. At the same time, education systems everywhere are increasingly turning to school choice as a means of expanding families' educational options and improving students' academic outcomes.[1] The confluence of these two trends—growing immigrant-origin student populations and school districts' greater reliance on school choice policies—has introduced a series of important new questions in the longstanding debates on equity in education.

Unaccompanied Minors sets out to examine the equity premise of New York City's compulsory high school choice policy by exploring the policy from the perspectives and experiences of three actors: district administrators, school-level personnel, and eighth-grade students and parents tasked with choosing high schools. The book started by identifying a series of assumptions underlying the choice policy that threaten its equity potential from the outset. First, the New York City Department of Education (NYCDOE) expects that all parents will be intimately involved in the high school search and decision-making process. Next, the district anticipates a high degree of school-level investment in preparing students and parents to knowledgably participate in high school choice. Finally, the policy assumes that all students will actively engage in a rigorous school search process, including attending city-wide and borough-based events, high school open houses and workshops, conducting online research, and relying on a network of family and school supports to make suitable high school selections.

Ethnographic observations and interviews with school personnel, students, and parents revealed a far different reality in terms of how the school choice policy gets implemented at the school level and how ethnically and socioeconomically diverse students and families actually participate in the choice process. For starters, NYCDOE put in place no oversight or accountability structures to ensure that middle schools are providing the information, support, and guidance that district administrators deem necessary or appropriate. As a result, schools already under tremendous pressure to meet academic performance targets and other benchmarks are prone to relegate school choice activities to low-priority status. In other words, students and parents at low-performing, high-needs middle schools like IS 725 receive minimal counseling or guidance from school personnel about the mechanics of the choice policy, how to access information about high schools, or which strategies to use to identify appropriate high school options.

Parents also exhibit a range of behaviors and child-rearing philosophies that challenge district administrators' ideas of typical or anticipated involvement in choice. Only the upper-middle-class white parents—a small minority of parents in the district—participated in high school choice in ways consistent with the district's assumptions. Conversely, low-income Latin American immigrant parents' views about child-rearing, their perspectives on the significance of "school quality," and their ideas about the appropriate division of labor between children and parents enacted in the context of high school choice were in diametric opposition to district expectations.

Parents' heterogeneous views about the importance of evaluating schools' academic outcomes and their varied degrees of engagement in school search activities highlight a fatal flaw in one of the choice policy's key theoretical underpinnings: the assumption that through choice, parents will exert influence over the educational marketplace and put pressure on schools to raise performance.[2] The situation in New York City contradicts this assumption in two ways. First, low-income Latin American immigrant parents indicated that they were unconcerned about a school's academic outcomes and did not encourage their children to consider this factor when making choices. As important, a severe undersupply of high performing high schools persists in New York City after more than a decade of extensive investment in choice. What is more, parents have been essentially sidelined in conversations about how to respond to underperforming schools. In fact, state- and district-level accountability measures and the associated sanctions for poor performance function as the primary mechanism for influencing schools; the impact of parental voices through school choice, if anything, has been largely symbolic.

Students' choice experiences varied dramatically in terms of their modes of participation, access to guidance and supports, and, most importantly, their likelihood of being matched to a high performing high school. Differences in students' engagement in choice strongly correlated with family background characteristics such as parental income, education, and nativity. My study revealed that students from higher income, more educated families tended to invest heavily in researching, evaluating, and selecting schools; had parents who lived up to NYCDOE's expectations of involvement; and benefited from an integrated network of supports, guidance, and consistent messages from peers, school personnel, and family members about which schools were acceptable, appropriate, and desirable. They used these resources to make informed decisions, prioritize high performing high schools, and gain access to the most competitive high schools. In other words, they engaged in *strategic choice*. By contrast, lower income, predominantly Latino immigrant-origin students and parents exhibited considerably less knowledge about or investment in the high school choice process. Consequently, these students had substantially less success in being matched to high performing high schools.

I contend that policies like school choice in New York City have the potential to accomplish even more than increasing students' and parents' ownership over their educational decisions and improving educational equity. The skills and strategies that can be honed through the process of choosing high schools in New York City—namely, conducting research, analyzing school performance and other data, weighing options, and ranking preferences—are in fact applicable to many other personal and professional experiences. Yet for this to occur, particularly among lower income, immigrant-origin youth, schools must play a more active role in guiding students and families through choice policies. This also means schools must work to facilitate students' development of strategic choice skills, tools, and knowledge that are relevant to negotiating a host of bureaucratic and competitive processes.

The section that follows presents a series of concrete policies, programs, and activities that school districts, schools, and community-based organizations can implement to better support all students and families in school choice, increase the equity potential of choice policies, and facilitate the development of transferable research, evaluation, and analytical tools. The recommendations emphasize greater district investment and school-level involvement in informing, educating, and advising students. They stem from a belief in the need to return to education policies that focus explicitly on the needs of disadvantaged populations or "redistributive equity" policies in order to genuinely pursue equity goals. Currently, the educational landscape is dominated by free-market policies that promote individual rights in education or excellence for all approaches that do not emphasize the specific needs of historically disenfranchised groups. New York City's high school choice policy is an illustrative example. Replacing one-size-fits-all policies with those that actively attempt to level the playing field represents the best chance for moving away from the rhetoric of choice and equity and toward the reality.

RECOMMENDATIONS TO INCREASE THE EQUITY POTENTIAL OF SCHOOL CHOICE

NYCDOE's approach to high school choice reflects a pervasive affliction of current school-reform efforts: equity-driven policies in theory that are poorly designed to achieve the goals of improving historically disadvantaged students' educational opportunities. Yet feasible solutions exist to each of the district's most serious missteps: the inadequate provision and dissemination of information, a lack of mandated school-based guidance, and faulty assumptions about parent involvement. Providing wider access to school choice publications, improving mechanisms for oversight and support of school-based guidance, and reallocating resources in order to respond to students' and parents' information and guidance needs are just some of the ways NYCDOE and other districts can rethink their approaches to policy formation and implementation.

Increased school-based support and guidance are essential to improve the equity potential of New York City's school choice policy. Students and families, particularly from low-income, immigrant-origin backgrounds, would benefit from instruction on the nuances of the application process, detailed information about the range of schools available, training on how to access school performance data, and personal school-based counseling sessions that pinpoint specific, appropriate school options. But this is only a first, small step toward a more equitable approach to school choice. Merely scheduling additional parent workshops and guidance sessions is insufficient to attack the complex underlying factors contributing to current choice outcomes. If parents are not thinking about or particularly concerned with their children's high school selections or if they do not understand the implications of different high school assignments (e.g., the dramatically reduced probability that their child will graduate from a high school with a 50 percent graduation rate compared to one with 85 percent or above), the additional outreach efforts may have minimal impact.

Unaccompanied Minors identifies a fundamental disconnect between low-income Latin American immigrant parents' parenting philosophies and the normative assumptions embedded within New York City's high school choice policy (and a host of other education policies in the United States). This finding pointed to the need for more explicit direction about what is and is not expected of parents and a thorough discussion of the potential consequences for children when parents do not live up to these expectations. Conversations about school-wide outcomes and why they may impact students' educational opportunities may also be required to establish some common ground. Such discussions can provide a space for parents and students to gain knowledge about how to negotiate different institutional relationships, environments, and processes. In this way, structured interactions between school personnel and families can promote the generation of valuable cultural capital and an *institutional compass*. Improved school choice practices that leverage choice into a broader developmental exercise could therefore have impacts far beyond immediate gains in the equitable distribution of high-quality educational opportunities.

To that end, the recommendations emphasize specific steps that district administrators and school personnel can take to support thoughtful, deliberate, decision making within and outside the context of school choice. The ideas and suggestions presented below are by no means comprehensive; instead, they are intended to serve as a starting point for discussion on how to transform perceptions and behaviors at each level of the system—from district administrators to individual students and families—so that school choice may actually function as a lever for greater educational access and equity. The proposed suggestions understand school choice policies as an opportunity for schools to help families learn how to be informed consumers and active participants in many different kinds of marketplaces. The proposals are grouped into three sections: (1) changes to district-level policies and practices to improve school choice; (2) school-level changes to increase equity through choice; and (3) ways to leverage school choice for broader knowledge and skill development. While these recommendations were developed with New York City's choice and accountability context in mind, they can be easily applied to other districts like New Orleans and Milwaukee with robust choice programs in place or to districts such as Chicago and Philadelphia that are rapidly transitioning to a portfolio model with expanded choice and reduced central-office oversight.

CHANGES TO DISTRICT-LEVEL POLICIES AND PRACTICES TO IMPROVE CHOICE

Improve Information Provision

Publish translated versions of school choice documents in print

NYCDOE must prioritize making available translated versions of all the essential school choice publications in printed format. Continued reliance on electronic documents constitutes a major impediment to many families' access to the most basic information about high school choice.

Create a stand-alone school choice advisory entity

To supplement the city-wide events and school-based activities, districts should consider developing a stand-alone entity dedicated to working with families on school choice. The borough enrollment offices currently operating across New York City have neither the capacity nor the mandate to do more than place students in open seats. The Family Resource Center in Cambridge, Massachusetts, offers a model example of how to provide support to parents in a controlled choice environment. Housed in a high school, the Family Resource Center has staff on hand to work individually with parents and students who, per district policy, are required to participate in a school lottery. Available year-round to advise new and existing residents, in-person counseling can be combined with online resources. New York City would need multiple family resource center sites across the five boroughs with bilingual staff in order to serve its large, linguistically diverse population. These centers could be dedicated to providing information and guidance about school choice at every level of schools (kindergarten through college) and could provide services beyond just school choice advisement.

Provide free school choice training for community-based organizations

School districts and individual schools are limited in the resources and personnel they have to dedicate to any particular task, and school choice is no exception. Community-based organizations working directly with students and families represent another potential partner for districts. Staff members at CBOs often have relationships with youth and adults who may be less likely to engage with school personnel, and they may interact with parents and students differently from school representatives. As a result, they could offer diverse perspectives on families' experiences with choice and with the education system in general. CBOs should also be offered training and materials about high school choice and encouraged to work with youth and parents in the community on choice, and wherever possible, be given subsidies and grants to do this work.

Establish Minimum Requirements for School-Based Activities

Currently, middle schools in New York City have full rein to decide the content of the information that will be disseminated to students and parents, how this information will be shared, when, and by whom. To get closer to its imagined version of choice that includes extensive school personnel guidance and support, NYCDOE must develop concise, realistic, and manageable instructions for middle school–based choice activities. In order to adequately prepare students and families for participation in high school choice, outreach activities should begin well before the start of students' eighth-grade year. Rather, schools should be required to organize events and workshops at each grade level (sixth, seventh, and eighth) so that by the time students actually have to fill out applications, they are knowledgeable and prepared. This mandate will help ensure that all students have access to at least some basic information and adult interaction relevant to choosing high schools during their middle school years.

Develop mandatory school choice training for school personnel

Obligatory school-based outreach and guidance to families about high school choice is only as good as the quality of the information and advice disseminated. NYCDOE should institute a series of mandatory workshops for school counselors, parent coordinators, or other school personnel responsible for working with families on high school choice. These workshops could serve multiple purposes: first, NYCDOE officials could model the kinds of informational and guidance activities they expect to see taking place at school for students and families at each grade level and ensure that school-based staff have the most up-to-date, accurate information about the choice process. The workshops could also provide a space for school personnel to exchange strategies, materials, and ideas about how best to engage and educate students and parents about the choice process based on their own experiences. Last, district administrators could use the workshops as an opportunity to clearly explain the new mandates on school information provision, articulate their expectations, and describe the oversight and accountability mechanisms.

Provide additional resources to high-need schools for school choice counseling

In schools like IS 725 with large low-income, immigrant student populations, school personnel are often the sole source of information that families have about school choice and many other education policies, programs, and opportunities. In order to adequately meet their information and guidance needs and to mitigate the impacts of imbalances in family resources and knowledge, districts should cover the cost of additional school personnel, overtime for guidance staff, and/or family outreach and engagement activities at each grade level in schools serving high-needs populations.

Create Mechanisms for Oversight and Accountability of School-Based Actions

District leadership must take decisive action to shift school leaders' and school personnel's view of the importance of high school choice and what they must do to help students and families knowledgeably engage in choice. This cannot occur without taking into account the pressures and influence of accountability systems. In order to ensure compliance with requirements in the current accountability-driven context, school evaluations should incorporate some assessment of fidelity of implementation of the choice policy. Measures of student and parent satisfaction with information and guidance received and public accountability such as releasing choice results and student performance in high schools are other ways to encourage middle schools to focus on the choice process.

Link information-provision requirements to accountability

For school leaders and personnel to take seriously any guidelines about school choice information provision, the guidelines must be linked to concrete mechanisms for oversight and accountability. Although educational evaluation has moved away from input-based assessments to a nearly exclusive focus on outcomes, one straightforward way to promote compliance with the requirements is to monitor how often, how much, and how well middle schools engage with students and families about high school choice. This could happen through a mandatory online reporting process combined with unannounced school visits by district representatives. Middle schools should not be held fully responsible for students' ultimate high school assignments since students' eligibility and their own preferences are the final determinants. Consequently, instituting benchmarks for informing students and families and meticulously checking to make sure that schools meet them could be a promising way for the district to broadcast the significance of these choice-related activities to school personnel. In light of the influence of accountability on quotidian school operations, district officials might also consider including a school choice compliance score in school-level evaluations to make these tasks correlated to larger measures of school performance.

Measure parent and student satisfaction with high school information and guidance

Compliance measures may yield little information about how well informed or well prepared school choice participants feel as a result of school outreach activities. Top-down guidelines about what and how information should be shared may also be out of touch with what students and parents want. Gathering data directly from the consumers is critical to determining the effectiveness of school-based efforts and identifying areas for improvement. A survey administered to eighth-grade students and parents that measures their satisfaction with the information they receive is one way to do this. A stand-alone survey could be administered to attendees after the conclusion of school-based activities or relevant questions could be added to the existing NYC School Survey already distributed to students and parents. This second option—including new questions on the NYC School Survey—would create another linkage between school choice and school accountability since survey results already count in a school's *Progress Report* grade.

Publish an annual report of each middle school's high school choice results

It has long been standard practice in many school districts for high schools to make public the list of colleges and universities that graduating seniors will be attending the following year. This form of public accountability can be a powerful way to stoke competition among high schools and motivate them to assist students in attempting to gain acceptance to well-regarded institutions. In districts like New York City where many middle schools actually compete for students as a result of the school choice landscape (including charter schools, magnet programs, and choice among traditional public schools), making these results widely known through an annual report might prompt middle schools to invest greater time and energy into working with students on high school choice. Specifically, it might motivate middle schools to help students identify and apply to the highest performing high schools to which they are eligible. Rising middle school students and parents might consider the high school choice results in their own middle school selections, thereby increasing the incentives for school personnel to invest time and energy.

Publish an annual report of middle school graduates'
high school performance and outcomes

The district should use public accountability tools to encourage the development of a school-wide culture geared toward high school preparedness and informed school choice. For example, students' high school performance (e.g., state test scores, graduation rates) could be publicly linked to the middle schools they attended—similar to the recent move to include the name of the teacher-preparation program attended on public teacher-evaluation reports.[3] This form of public accountability could in turn exert pressure on middle schools to take seriously the endeavor of preparing students for high school academically as well as socially and emotionally. Districts might also sponsor competitions for creative school choice awareness and outreach efforts, fund pilot school-based programs to develop new school choice tools, or find other ways to recognize outstanding achievements in the realm of school choice preparation and high school readiness.

SCHOOL-LEVEL CHANGES TO INCREASE EQUITY THROUGH CHOICE

The power and obligation to improve school choice policies and procedures, including information provision and guidance, do not reside solely with district leadership. On the contrary, school principals, teachers, counselors, and staff must be at the very heart of efforts to identify and better respond to students' needs for instruction and assistance in negotiating school choice and developing the associated skills, sensibilities, and habits.

Prioritize School Choice Counseling

Among the vast array of tasks that middle school personnel must complete vis-à-vis high school choice, some require specialized knowledge and skills while others consist of little more than administrative paper-shuffling. Rather than assigning trained school counselors to oversee the entire enterprise, principals should consider dividing the tasks based on type of expertise needed. Volunteers, paraprofessionals, or other staff members can be asked to distribute copies of the *High School Directory*, distribute and collect application forms, and input completed applications into the online system. This division of labor would free up guidance counselors to spend more time engaged in individual counseling sessions and parent workshops, which they tend to enjoy more and are likely to be more beneficial to students.

By the same token, if the prominence of school choice is elevated through district-led initiatives and mandates like those proposed above, principals may ask school counselors to dedicate more time to working with students and families. One way to manage these additional demands is to carefully review how guidance counselors are currently spending their time and determine which responsibilities can be shifted to other school personnel. Replacing some of the administrative tasks with more counseling-intensive ones may increase job satisfaction among counselors as well as provide vital support to students during a difficult period of adolescent transition and development. This suggestion is consistent with those advanced by other scholars and advocates who have lamented the tendency for school leadership to "relegate school counselors to roles such as quasi-administrator, registrar, and clerk . . . [which] are in diametric opposition to the roles for which school counselors are trained."[4]

Create a School Culture Focused on Thoughtful Engagement in High School Choice

A positive "college-going culture" has been increasingly recognized as a powerful contributor to improving high school students' college readiness and access.[5] Middle school leaders should learn from successful examples of strong college-going cultures in high schools and translate some of the effective practices to their own settings to promote thoughtful engagement in high school choice as part of the middle school's culture and identity. Many of the traditional metrics used to evaluate the strength of a school's "college-going culture" are inapplicable when assessing a "school choice culture."[6] Yet a number of the school-level structures and building blocks identified as necessary to establish a "strong college-going culture" are easily transferrable to the middle school/high school choice context. For example, researchers have cited a central role for school personnel in building and sustaining the culture through provision of college-related guidance and planning assistance during and outside of class time, using a college preparatory curriculum, and communicating high expectations for students' college attendance.[7] This is in addition to having well-publicized norms and goals for college attendance and providing associated information and guidance supports. In schools with strong college-going cultures, teachers and other staff are encouraged to expand their professional identities and duties beyond strictly academic instruction and take personal pride in helping facilitate students' successful transition to postsecondary education.

When developing the middle school's discourse and goals vis-à-vis high school choice, school leaders must consider outcomes beyond the number of students admitted to the most competitive (specialized and screened) high schools, since not every student will be eligible for admission. Rather, a positive school culture around choice may include recognition of students' efforts to actively engage in choice activities and awards for demonstrating superior knowledge about the choice process and educational options. Schools may consider sponsoring competitions with prizes for developing innovative school search tools and strategies; create opportunities for within- and cross-grade peer mentorship about high school choice; and work to brand itself as a school with unique institutional practices and expertise around high school choice to attract prospective middle school students. Acknowledgment of students' success in obtaining admission to their desired high schools as both an individual and school-wide achievement could also help cultivate a sense of community spirit around school choice.

Promote a Shared Choice Experience Among Peers

All students, regardless of their achievement level or track, have the potential to develop a sense of shared mission when faced with the task of choosing high schools. Schools should build on their existing structures to foment this feeling among students. They can do so by converting the classroom, home room, advisory group, or other entities into a space for mutual support, information-sharing, and norm construction among classmates about what smart, appropriate high school choices look like. This happened organically for students in the gifted and talented track at IS 725, but administrators and teachers can do a number of things to stimulate something similar for all students. Group activities and discussion about how to access information, which school characteristics matter, and why school selections are made could convert these existing entities into a fruitful support structure for students who may have few resources outside of the school building with whom to discuss and strategize. It may not be possible for all students or classrooms to generate a highly focused *multiply reinforced orientation* like the gifted and talented track students did or for a restrictive norm to guide all students' choices. Yet there are many potential benefits of cultivating an esprit de corps among classmates around the act of choosing high schools. They can range from dissuading students from considering the lowest performing high schools to fortifying social and emotional bonds to peers during a critical developmental stage. Efforts to generate classroom-level norms, practices, and standards about high school choice can bolster a broader, school-wide commitment and campaign focused on thoughtful school choice engagement described above.

Dedicate homeroom or class time for students to share high school–related information

Students should be asked periodically to report something they have learned about the high school choice process or about specific high schools and programs of interest to them. For this exercise to yield maximum pedagogical benefit to students and their classmates, students should be asked to explain how they accessed the information they are sharing and to articulate their reasons for liking or disliking a particular school. Allocating time for such discussions symbolically demonstrates the importance of high school choice and provides opportunities for information exchange and skill-building.

Divide students into teams and assign them information-gathering responsibilities

Team-building activities that result in information generation could increase the sense of connectedness among smaller groups of students and help them develop a sense of ownership over the process of learning about and identifying school options. Assigned tasks may include finding out open-house dates for high schools in a certain geographic area, generating a list of high schools with certain admissions criteria or characteristics, or identifying middle school alumni at different high schools who would be willing to speak to the group about their high school experiences.

Facilitate conversations among students about desirable school characteristics

Discussions about the range of school characteristics that could be considered when selecting high schools, how to weigh their relative importance when making decisions, and how to access information about these characteristics could go a long way toward increasing students' communal knowledge about schools and choices. Consensus should not necessarily be the goal of these conversations, particularly since students will be qualified for different schools and programs based on academic achievement. However, agreement about certain schools that should be avoided or targeted data points that should be considered (including size, graduation rates, college readiness, or other academic indicators) would help establish a baseline standard for students at all performance levels.

Fuel competition among classes to motivate students to engage in choice activities

Create incentives for students to attend open houses, city-wide or borough-wide fairs, or to participate in other choice-related activities in greater numbers or as a group. Rewards could be offered for classes that attend the most events or gather the most detailed information, thereby enhancing class unity around choice.

Help Students Develop an Institutional Compass for High School Choice Navigation

An instructive roadmap, or *institutional compass*, is essential for school choice participants to convert ideas and desires into effective action—in the form of a purposefully completed application and, ultimately, admission to a desired high school. Schools are well positioned to provide these supports to students (and even their family members), offer them instruction on how to use an institutional compass, and develop structured opportunities to put it to use. Mini-lessons on discrete elements of the institutional compass could be included in any number of the class- or school-wide activities suggested above to cultivate a school choice culture and positive peer relationships. Lessons may range from how to search for the information you want to how to assess the likelihood of admission and improve your chances for acceptance by different schools. These discussions could also be made part of individual student/family meetings with school personnel. Because an institutional compass used for navigating high school choice in New York City could be a useful tool in many contexts, an emphasis on practical skill-building rather than direct instruction is critical. This means facilitating simulations, exercises, and hands-on learning experiences in conjunction with lectures, PowerPoint presentations, or other traditional forms of instruction.

Tap middle school alumni to serve as high school ambassadors

Current high school students are a vastly underutilized resource for enhancing school-based support for high school choice. They can also be instrumental in helping students develop an institutional compass for high school choice and beyond. Middle schools should tap their alumni to provide honest, relevant information to rising ninth-graders, not just about which high school to choose but how to prepare for the transition to high school more generally. It is common practice in many high schools already to invite the previous year's seniors to return to speak with juniors and seniors about their first-year college experiences. A similar model could be adopted by middle schools in places where high school choice exists. Through an assembly, an afterschool event, or classroom visits, eighth-grade students would have an opportunity to speak directly with current high school students, ask questions, and potentially be exposed to a wider range of school options or new strategies to best position themselves for acceptance to their desired high school. Ideally, the high school students would come from similar backgrounds to the middle school students so that questions of "fitting in" and comfort in an unknown environment may be more easily addressed.

In the age of social media and unparalleled Internet connectivity, middle schools could also use a host of existing web-based platforms to facilitate connections between current middle school students and recent graduates. For example, school counselors could set up a dedicated Facebook page for discussion about high schools. Or, current ninth-grade students could be invited to write a blog about their experiences at different high schools across the city and answer questions provided by middle school students. Middle school students could take the lead in developing an alumni engagement strategy and determining which web-based tools to use for these purposes, and this activity could serve as yet another way to involve them in the high school choice endeavor overall.

Engage Parents in High School Choice

Recommendations for school-level action so far have centered on ways to bolster positive peer relationships and a thoughtful school-wide choice culture, including active personnel involvement to promote *strategic choice* behaviors among students. Both sets of recommendations deal with actions taking place inside the school building where, in theory, it is easier to ensure consistent messaging about informed decision making—a critical ingredient for the production of a *multiply reinforced orientation*. By contrast, family participation, the third leg of the stool of strategic choice, operates externally to school operations. School administrators should therefore make it a priority to engage directly with families to understand their perspectives on choosing schools.

Learn about families' perspectives on schools and choice to ensure consistent messages

School administrators should solicit parents' ideas about important school characteristics and incorporate them into school-based communications to students in order to maintain as much uniformity as possible in the advice and information students receive at home and at school vis-à-vis choosing appropriate high schools. Reaching a consensus between school personnel and families about what constitutes a "good" choice may neither be desirable nor attainable; rather, as in the case of establishing classroom norms, a more reasonable goal might be to come to a basic agreement about which data points to review and what minimum standards (geographic, academic, other) must be met for a school to warrant consideration. Above all, it is crucial to avoid situations in which students receive contradictory advice from school and home about how to make choices.

The benefits associated with eliciting parents' feedback and ideas about school choice may extend beyond just ensuring that students hear consistent messages. Low-income and immigrant parents frequently feel alienated by school personnel, disrespected, and undervalued.[8] If school administrators start the choice conversation with parents as a listening exercise and demonstrate interest in understanding parents' perspectives, an opportunity for a different kind of home-school collaboration may emerge. Instead of one-way, school-led instruction about what effective or appropriate choice-making looks like, school personnel and families can co-construct culturally responsive definitions of reasonable, appropriate, and quality choices. This may lead to improved understanding and communication across a host of educational areas, not just school choice.

Build choice awareness activities into existing school-sponsored parent events

Encouraging parents to attend traditional school events can often be a challenging task. Rather than making additional demands on parents' time with new events, school administrators should consider adding high school choice–focused activities and information to existing events. Below are some ideas about how to accomplish this:

- Build time into annual "back-to-school night" events for discussion of high school choice with parents.
- Include high school choice as a required topic during parent-teacher meetings for eighth-grade students.
- Host parent–guidance counselor meetings for seventh- and eighth-grade parents where high school choice is a focal topic.
- Sponsor free workshops, classes, and events of interest to parents at the school site (e.g., English classes, computer lit-

eracy classes, exercise classes, free tax-return completion) and use time during one or more sessions to discuss high school choice.

Schools must strike a delicate balance between lecturing and listening so that parents feel like partners in the choice endeavor. Efforts to engage and inform parents about school choice provide a vital opportunity to help parents understand its importance, learn how to negotiate the system, and ultimately feel empowered to participate in this and other aspects of their children's educational journeys.

WAYS TO LEVERAGE SCHOOL CHOICE FOR BROADER KNOWLEDGE AND SKILL DEVELOPMENT

For students to maximally benefit from the experience of choosing high schools, school personnel must embrace the notion that it can yield much more than just a high school placement. School leaders and counselors must first understand the parallels between the skills needed to effectively participate in high school choice (e.g., identify appropriate high school options, distinguish among them, and make informed decisions based on some overarching goal or criteria) and what young adults need to successfully participate in any number of other educational, developmental, economic, or civic activities (e.g., choosing colleges, finding employment, deciding which candidate to support). This requires school leaders to recast the conversation in their schools about what high school choice means and why it matters and make the necessary changes to staff and time allocations to give it the attention it deserves. School counselors should be encouraged to use school choice activities as a platform to advise students and families more broadly and to facilitate the knowledge and skill-building that high school choice allows for. With the proper investment in developing choice skills, school choice policies may live up to its promise of serving as an engine of equity promotion.

*Draw parallels between the mechanics of high school
and college choice*

Although the actual application procedures for high schools and colleges differ substantially, the search stage is quite similar. School personnel should use high school choice as a platform to discuss the college search and application process and the significance of an effective *institutional compass* for negotiating choice at both levels of education. School counselors, teachers, or other staff could conduct side-by-side comparisons of high school and college choice and ask students to research colleges alongside high schools of interest. High school juniors and seniors could be invited to speak to eighth-grade students and offer their own reflections on the differences and parallels between the application experiences. In the end, a school-based effort to facilitate students' development of knowledge and skills to extract maximum benefit from bureaucratic and competitive processes like school choice could pay large dividends. Doing so may help establish a critical link between secondary and postsecondary education by demonstrating concretely how it can be an interconnected, continuous path.

Connect high school and college choice with career aspirations

Many eighth-grade students and their parents are unable to name a New York City high school, let alone a college or university, they would like to attend. However, it is likely much easier for them to articulate career goals and aspirations. School personnel or others leading discussions about high school choice should work backward from students' or parents' desired careers. They could identify degree requirements of different careers (or better yet, assign students and parents this task), map career requirements to the degree and course offerings at different educational institutions (two-year versus four-year, technical schools, etc.), and ultimately make explicit the connection between college and high school choices. Students and parents should also be introduced to college

admissions requirements, specifically high school course requirements in core academic subjects, as early as eighth grade so they
can begin to chart out their academic schedules and paths prior to
entering high school.

*Identify available high school–level data and information
relevant for college choices*

Differences in students' and families knowledge about high school
course taking and college admissions requirements, application
procedures, financial aid, and even the relationship between postsecondary credentials and careers contribute to uneven college
application, enrollment, and completion rates across racial/ethnic
and income groups.[9] These patterns have roots that stretch as far
back as middle school, if not earlier. Providing explicit instruction
to students (and parents) about high school–level data points associated with a student's college readiness and access (e.g., AP and
advanced math and science course offerings, school-wide average
SAT scores, college admissions results) and how to access them
may yield multiple benefits. First, school choosers may now consider these academic indicators when selecting high schools. Second, they might understand the association between high school
placement and college opportunities.

Disparities in educational access and attainment in New York
City and nationwide make clear that the promise of school choice
to promote greater equity has yet to be realized. Growing income
stratification has emerged as a major cause for concern among
politicians, policy makers, and citizens, and the implications of increasing economic stratification for education are far-reaching.[10]
The recommendations above represent only a small slice of the
possibilities for transforming school choice policies and practices
into a catalyst for greater educational and social equity. There is a
serious need for research that tests different school-, family-, and
community-level interventions to help students and parents strategically select schools in the context of choice plans and build
knowledge and skills that can be lifelong assets in many different

arenas. First, however, school districts must be willing to assume a larger, more direct role in informing, guiding, and supporting students and families—particularly the most disadvantaged ones—in order to lay the groundwork for an equity agenda to be legitimately pursued.

A SHIFT IN PERSPECTIVE

What is happening in New York City and in education policy more generally is not unique. Emphasis on individual autonomy and responsibility has long reigned supreme in the United States. Limits to governmental involvement in private or local matters have been erected and ardently defended, resulting in a weak public commitment to government intervention or to direct efforts aimed at redistributive equity. Although redistributive equity policies were commonplace in the 1960s and early 1970s (e.g., Title I of the federal Elementary and Secondary Education Act, affirmative action, and Project Head Start), in the midst of rising fiscal deficits, major cuts in education funding, and the release of *A Nation at Risk* in 1983, the focus shifted from the rights of disenfranchised groups to the rights of all individuals to receive a high-quality education.[11] By removing the rights and needs of underserved groups from the spotlight and instead describing educational rights in individual terms, rewarding individual merit replaced access as a priority. The persistent inequities plaguing many choice initiatives are a consequence of this move away from a commitment to redistributive equity.

Establishing a more direct role for public agencies in correcting historic imbalances and inequities across a range of public and social sectors could produce numerous benefits. A coalition of experts in the fields of social welfare, health, housing, civil rights, and education working with the "Broader, Bolder Approach to Education" campaign argues forcefully for a reenvisioned concept of schools that vastly expands their reach and transforms them into a primary base from which diverse youth and community development efforts can be launched.[12] Their call for greater school involvement and services is linked directly to an "expanded concept of education" that parallels many of the ideas presented in this book. Such an education "pays attention not only to basic academic skills and cognitive growth narrowly defined, but to development of the whole person, including physical health, character, social development, and non-academic skills . . . It assigns value to the new knowledge and skills that young people need to become effective participants in a global environment, including citizenship, creativity, and the ability to respect and work with persons from different backgrounds."[13] Such fundamental shifts in ideology and ideas about what constitutes education mark a crucial step. This ideological change must be accompanied by policy and behavioral changes in order to progress toward the social and educational equity that could be possible in schools and society today.

---■■■---

Methodology

OBSERVATIONS OF CITY-WIDE HIGH SCHOOL CHOICE EVENTS

Each year, the New York City Department of Education hosts a series of city-wide and borough-based workshops and fairs to inform families about high school choice. As part of this study, ethnographic observations were conducted at ten city-wide high school choice events held between June 2008 and December 2010 at different school locations in Queens, Brooklyn, the Bronx, and Manhattan. Events included open parent meetings, workshops about how to fill out the high school application, and the city-wide and borough-based high school fairs hosted by NYCDOE district and borough representatives. These observations provided insight into the various district-wide communication efforts, NYCDOE officials' expectations of choice participants, and their recommended strategies for making school selections.

DOCUMENT ANALYSIS

NYCDOE publishes various printed and electronic materials about the high school choice process. These include a 600-page *Directory of New York City Public High Schools* that is distributed to each rising eighth-grade student and a number of short brochures and pamphlets that summarize different school types and offer tips to parents about how to work with their children to select high schools. These documents were analyzed in terms of the type of media used (e.g., electronic versus print), their accessibility (language, technological requirements), and the content of the information provided, namely: the criteria emphasized in how to determine appropriate school selections; suggested activities for parents and students; and the expectations, both articulated and implied, of parents' roles in the choice process. The table below provides a brief description of the main high school choice–related materials produced by NYCDOE and analyzed for this study.

High School Choice Publications from the New York City Department of Education

Publication	Content	Printed/ Online/ Both	Language(s)	Length
Directory of New York City High Schools	Dedicated page for each high school with description of programs, features, admissions requirements	Both	Printed only in English. Online in Arabic, Bengali, Chinese, Haitian Creole, Korean, Russian, Spanish, Urdu, and English	600 pages
High Schools at a Glance	High schools and programs listed in tabular format with five features identified: program name, program code, interest area, selection method, page number in *High School Directory*	Both	Printed only in English. Online in Arabic, Bengali, Chinese, Haitian Creole, Korean, Russian, Spanish, Urdu, and English	44 pages
Choosing a High School: Information for Middle School Students	Contains various "decision-making tools" including a "student interest inventory," summaries of the types of high schools, screen shot of *High School Directory* page, sample application form, and "special strategies" for parents	Both	Printed only in English. Online in Arabic, Bengali, Chinese, Haitian Creole, Korean, Russian, Spanish, Urdu, and English	20 pages

Publication	Content	Printed/ Online/ Both	Language(s)	Length
Making Choices: A High School Admissions Handbook	Summary of choice process, exercises to help students identify interests and skills, list of questions to consider when making choices, sample *High School Directory* page, overview of selection methods	Both	Printed only in English. Online in Arabic, Bengali, Chinese, Haitian Creole, Korean, Russian, Spanish, Urdu, and English	14 pages
Specialized High School Student Handbook	Information about the specialized high schools, including programs, admission procedures, sample tests with test-taking tips, and a calendar of important dates	Both	Printed only in English. Online in Arabic, Bengali, Chinese, Haitian Creole, Korean, Russian, Spanish, Urdu, and English	111 pages
High School Admissions FAQs	Answers to seventeen most frequently asked questions about high school choice	Printed	English	4 pages
How to Navigate the City-wide Fair	Bulleted list of suggestions for making the most out of the city-wide high school fair	Both	English	3 pages
Making Choices: Finding a High School That's Right for You: Screened Programs	Summary of data points that screened programs use to evaluate candidates and description of additional activities (e.g., interview, portfolio, writing sample, diagnostic assessment)	Printed	English	1 page
Making Choices: Finding a High School That's Right for You: Performing Arts High Schools	Description of performing arts high schools and various activities required for admission. Recommendations for preparing for visual arts audition, portfolio, drama/theater audition, music audition, and dance audition	Printed	English	5 pages

NYCDOE School Performance and Accountability Reports

Report	Content
Annual School Report Card	Annual publication produced by New York State that includes school demographics and performance data such as results on state examinations and graduation rates.
Progress Report	Report grades each school with an A, B, C, D, or F based on student progress (60%), student performance (25%), and school environment (15%). Scores are based on comparing results from one school to a peer group of up to forty schools with the most similar student population and to all schools city-wide.
Learning Environment Survey (now called *NYC School Survey*)	Survey administered to all students, parents, and teachers in grades 6–12. Questions designed to assess respondents' opinions about a school's academic expectations, communication, engagement, safety, and respect. Survey results contribute 10–15% of a school's *Progress Report* grade (the exact contribution to the *Progress Report* is dependent on school type).
Quality Review	Rating and report based on two- or three-day school visit to each NYCDOE school conducted by experienced educator. During the review, the external evaluator visits classrooms, talks with school leaders, and uses a rubric to evaluate how well the school is organized to support student achievement. After the site visit, the school receives a *Quality Review* rating and report that is published on the NYCDOE website.

ETHNOGRAPHIC OBSERVATIONS AT IS 725

Between September 2008 and June 2010, I engaged in over four hundred hours of fieldwork at IS 725 where I observed in detail how school personnel implemented the high school choice policy. Specifically, I was interested in understanding who was responsible for overseeing high school choice at the school level, what resources were allocated to informing students and parents about how the process worked, where it fell among the school leadership's priorities, and how school personnel felt about the high school choice process and their roles in it. I spent much of my time shadowing the five guidance counselors while they engaged in choice-related activities such as distributing applications and conducting presentations for groups of students. I also conducted informal interviews with each guidance counselor and observed his/her interactions with students who sought advice or assistance with the application. Finally, I met with the principal on at least five occasions to learn more about his goals for the school and interacted with other administrators, school support staff, and eighth-grade teachers on a regular basis.

INTERVIEWS

NYCDOE administrators

A joint semi-structured interview was conducted with two senior administrators who worked in the Office of Student Enrollment and Planning Operations (OSEPO) at the New York City Department of Education. At the time of the study, OSEPO oversaw the high school choice process, developed the school choice policies and procedures, and published related informational materials. The interview focused on the OSEPO representatives' goals for the choice policy and their expectations of the roles and responsibilities of the central district office, middle school principals and guidance counselors, and eighth-grade students and parents in the choice process.

Student interviews

A purposive sample of forty-six students who demonstrated diversity in terms of nativity (first generation immigrant, second generation, or African American/third generation or higher); academic achievement; academic track; birth order (first and not first in family to attend high school in New York City); and country of origin/parents' country of origin participated in one-on-one semi-structured interviews about their high school choice experiences. Students were interviewed in their preferred language (English or

Spanish), and the interviews, which lasted from thirty to forty-five minutes, took place during students' lunch periods or after school in a private room. The first interviews were conducted in early December, after students had turned in their completed high school applications, and continued until late May, after students had received their first-round high school matches.

The final sample of students who participated in interviews included thirteen first-generation students from Latin America and the Spanish-speaking Caribbean and twelve second-generation children of Latin American and Caribbean immigrant parents. Eight of the first-generation students were female, and seven were the first person in their family to participate in high school choice in New York City. This group also comprised seven students classified as "high performing" (based on grades that would qualify them for acceptance to most screened schools or programs) and six "low performers" (based on grades that would make them ineligible for any screened school or program). The countries of origin represented by first-generation student interviewees included the Dominican Republic, Ecuador, El Salvador, Mexico, and Colombia. The second-generation Latino student interview sample was composed of five females and seven males. Only four of these students were the first in their family to participate in high school choice, and there were twice as many low performing students (eight) as high performers (four). In addition to students of Dominican, Mexican, Ecuadoran, and Colombian descent, this group also included the son of Peruvian immigrant parents.

Fourteen African American or third-generation or higher students participated in interviews about high school choice. The sample included ten female students and four males, and eleven of them were not the first in their family to go through the high school choice process. Five of the African American/third-generation or higher students were considered "high performers," and nine were "low performers." The final subgroup of interview participants comprised seven students in the gifted and talented track. Six female and one male students in this track were interviewed, and they were all classified as high performers. Five of these students were the first in their family to participate in high school choice, and their parents came from India, Bangladesh, China, Pakistan, and the United States.

During the interviews, students were asked a series of questions about their understanding of how the high school choice process works and how they learned about it. They were also asked to identify the high schools they listed on their applications and to explain their rationale for the schools they selected. Finally, I inquired about parents' and family members' involvement in the choice process and their role relative to their parents' in decision making and asked them to identify the people who most strongly influenced their school selections. Students who were interviewed

Sampling Matrix for Student Interviews

	1st in Family to Go to High School in NYC		Not 1st in Family to Go to High School in NYC	
	High Performer	Low Performer	High Performer	Low Performer
1st Generation	3 (DR, EC, EL)	4 (EL, DR, MX)	4 (COL, EC, DR)	2 (DR, MX)
	2F, 1M	3F, 1M	3F, 1M	2M
2nd Generation	2 (DR, MX)	2 (MX)	3 (MX, EC, DR)	5 (DR, COL, EC, PE)
	1F, 1M	1F, 1M	1F, 2M	2F, 3M
African American / 3rd Generation	2F (US)	1M (US)	3F (US)	5F, 3M (US)
Gifted & Talented	5 (IN, BE, CH, US)		2 (BE, PK)	
	4F, 1M		2F	

Note: The top row indicates the students' or families' countries of origin. The second row indicates gender. Country codes: BE = Bangladesh, CH = China, COL = Colombia, DR = Dominican Republic, EC = Ecuador, EL = El Salvador, IN = India, MX = Mexico, PE = Peru, PK = Pakistan, US = United States, VZ = Venezuela. F represents female students, M represents male students.

after they had received their high school assignments were asked about their satisfaction with their high school match and asked to describe their feelings about going to high school generally.

Parent interviews

The sample of parent interview participants comprised twenty-four Latin American immigrant parents and eleven White upper middle class parents of eighth grade students enrolled in three different middle schools. The majority of Latin American immigrant parents came from Mexico (N=9), the Dominican Republic (N=7), and Ecuador (N=6) reflecting the broader population at IS 725. These participants included both parents with older children who had been through the choice process before (N=9) and those for whom this was the first time choosing high schools in New York City (N=15).

Upper-middle-class white parents were recruited from three Manhattan middle schools with relatively large white student populations (at least 30%) and low proportions of students who qualified for free lunch (50% or below). Nearly all the upper-middle-class parents had advanced degrees and worked in high-paying, professional industries such as finance and law, although

Sampling Matrix for Latin American Immigrant Parent Interviews

Child		Interview Participant			
		Mother	Father	Both Parents	TOTAL
1st Generation	Girl	1MX, 1EC, 2DR	1EC	1DR	6
	Boy	2EC, 2MX, 1DR, 1EL	1DR, 1MX		8
2nd Generation	Girl	1EC, 1DR, 1MX, 1VZ			4
	Boy	3MX, 1DR, 1EC		1MX	6
TOTAL		19	3	2	24

Note: Country codes: DR = Dominican Republic, EC = Ecuador, EL = El Salvador, MX = Mexico, VZ = Venezuela

Sampling Matrix for White Middle- and Upper-Middle-Class Parent
Interviews

Child		Interview Participant		Totals		
		Mother	Father	Girls	Boys	By MS
MS 1 (Manhattan)	Girl	0	1	1	0	
	Boy	4	3	0	7	8
MS 2 (Manhattan)	Girl	1	0	1	0	
	Boy	0	0	0	0	1
MS 3 (Manhattan)	Girl	2	0	2	0	
	Boy	0	0	0	0	2
TOTAL		7	4	4	7	11

Note: Column totals show the number of mothers (N=7) and fathers (N=4) who participated in interviews. Additionally, more parents of eighth-grade boys (N=7) were interviewed than parents of girls (N=4). The final column calculates the distribution of interview participants by middle school. The largest number of parents had children enrolled at MS1 in Manhattan (N=8) followed by MS3 (N=2) and MS2 (N=1).

there were teachers, artists, and stay-at-home mothers among them as well. These parents could be classified as belonging to the upper middle class according to Blau and Duncan's widely used index of occupational status hierarchies and their relationship to the social class structure in the United States. Roughly half the upper-middle-class white parents had prior experience with the high school choice process, and a disproportionate number of parents of male eighth-grade students were represented in the sample (N = 7).

A standard protocol was used in all parent interviews. The protocol was designed to elicit information from parents about their role in choosing high schools in New York City, the specific steps they took to identify high schools and make school selections, and their sources of information. I also asked parents to name the most helpful information sources, to describe the division of labor between them and their child with regard to choosing high schools, and to discuss their overall experience with and ideas about the high school application process in New York City. The semi-structured format of the interviews allowed for unscripted follow-up questions and probes to be asked in response to what emerged in the course of the interview.

All interviews were coded and analyzed using the Atlas.ti qualitative analysis software. A first reading brought to the surface repeated, prominent, or puzzling topics and identified broad categories of meaning both within and across parent and student subgroups. Stage two of my analysis consisted of highlighting the text, examining how topics, categories, and themes related to each other, and determining which ideas required deeper consideration. In the final phase, the most powerful themes and patterns were analyzed with the goal of succinctly capturing the underlying stories and identifying the broad theoretical implications of the data. I revisited the high school choice narratives of student-parent dyads and reviewed the analysis previously carried out to see if any additional topics and themes were suggested that could further extend the findings from interview data.

NOTES

INTRODUCTION

1. Jeanne Batalova and Alicia Lee, "Frequently Requested Statistics on Immigrants and Immigration in the United States," *Migration Policy Institute*, www.migration information.org/USfocus/display.cfm?ID=886#2 (accessed March 25, 2012); William J. Hussar and Tabitha M. Bailey, *Projections of Education Statistics to 2018*, U.S. Department of Education, National Center for Education Statistics, NCES 2009-062 (Washington, DC: Government Printing Office, 2009).

2. Population Reference Bureau, *Analysis of Data from the U.S. Census Bureau, Census 2000 Supplementary Survey, 2001 Supplementary Survey, 2002 through 2011 American Community Survey*, http://datacenter.kidscount.org/data/acrossstates/Default .aspx (accessed March 1, 2013).

3. Anthony P. Carnevale, Nicole Smith, and Jeff Strohl, *Help Wanted: Projections of Jobs and Education Requirements through 2018 Technical Report* (Washington, DC: Georgetown Center on Education and the Workforce, 2010); Lawrence F. Katz and Claudia Goldin, *The Race Between Education and Technology* (Cambridge, MA: Harvard University Press, 2008); U.S. Department of Labor, Bureau of Labor Statistics, *Employment and Earnings January 2010*, www.bls.gov/cps/cpsa2009.pdf (accessed March 4, 2010).

4. Linda Levine, *The U.S. Income Distribution and Mobility: Trends and International Comparisons* (Washington, DC: Congressional Research Service Report 7-5700, 2012); Emmanuel Saez, "Striking It Richer: The Evolution of Top Incomes in the United States (Updated with 2011 Estimates)," http://elsa.berkeley.edu/~saez/ saez-UStopincomes-2011.pdf (accessed March 3, 2013).

5. Sean F. Reardon, "The Widening Achievement Gap between the Rich and the Poor: New Evidence and Possible Explanations," in *Whither Opportunity? Rising Inequality, Schools, and Children's Life Chances*, ed. Gregory J. Duncan and Richard J. Murnane (New York: Russell Sage Foundation, 2011), 91–116; David S. Kirk and Robert J. Sampson, "Crime and the Production of Safe Schools," in *Whither Opportunity? Rising Inequality, Schools, and Children's Life Chances*, eds., Gregory J. Duncan and Richard J. Murnane (New York: Russell Sage Foundation, 2011), 397–418; Martha J. Bailey and Susan Dynarski, "Inequality in Postsecondary Education," in *Whither Opportunity? Rising Inequality, Schools, and Children's Life Chances*, ed. Gregory J. Duncan and Richard J. Murnane (New York: Russell Sage Foundation, 2011), 117–131.

6. Thomas D. Snyder and Sally A. Dillow, *Digest of Education Statistics, 2010,* U.S. Department of Education, National Center for Education Statistics, NCES 2011-015 (Washington, DC: Government Printing Office, 2011); Susan Aud et al., *The Condition of Education 2011,* U.S. Department of Education, National Center for Education Statistics, NCES 2011-033 (Washington, DC: Government Printing Office, 2011); Bailey and Dynarski, "Inequality," 2011.

7. Patricia Gándara and Frances Contreras, *The Latino Education Crisis: The Consequences of Failed Social Policies* (Cambridge, MA: Harvard University Press, 2009); Carola Suárez-Orozco, Marcelo M. Suárez-Orozco, and Irina Todorova, *Learning a New Land: Immigrant Students in American Society* (Cambridge, MA: The Belknap Press of Harvard University, 2008); Marcelo M. Suárez-Orozco and Carolyn Sattin, "Introduction: Learning in the Global Era," in *Learning in the Global Era: International Perspectives on Globalization and Education,* ed. Marcelo M. Suárez-Orozco (Berkeley, CA: University of California Press and Ross Institute, 2007), 1–41.

8. Population Research Bureau, *Analysis of Data,* 2012; Richard Fry and Jeffrey S. Passel, *Latino Children: A Majority Are U.S.-Born Offspring of Immigrants* (Washington, DC: Pew Hispanic Center, 2009).

9. Center for Education Reform, *Charter School Law.* www.edreform.com/issues/choice-charter-schools/laws-legislation (accessed March 5, 2012); Education Commission of the States, *Open Enrollment: 50-State Report,* http://mb2.ecs.org/reports/Report.aspx?id=268 (accessed March 25, 2012).

10. For research on variation in voluntary school choice participation rates by family socioeconomic status, see Douglas Archibald, *Magnet Schools, Voluntary Desegregation, and Public Choice Theory: Limits and Possibilities in a Big City School System* (Madison, WI: University of Wisconsin Press, 1998); David E. Campbell, Martin R. West, and Paul E. Peterson, "Participation in a National, Means-Tested Voucher Program, *Journal of Policy Analysis and Management,* 24 no. 3 (2005): 523-541; David J. Fleming, Joshua M. Cowen, John F. Witte, and Patrick J. Wolf, "Similar Students, Different Choices: Who Uses a School Voucher in an Otherwise Similar Population of Students?" *Education and Urban Society* available Online First at http://eus.sagepub.com/content/early/2013/12/17/0013124513511268.full.pdf+html; John F. Witte, *The Market Approach to Education; An Analysis of America's First Voucher Program* (Princeton, NJ: Princeton University Press, 2000); Ellen Goldring and Charles S. Hausman, "Reasons for Parental Choice of Urban Schools," *Journal of Education Policy* 4, no. 5 (1999): 469–490. For a discussion of school choice and "cream skimming" of higher income, higher performing students, see Edward B. Fiske and Helen F. Ladd, *When Schools Compete: A Cautionary Tale* (Washington, DC: Brookings Institution, 2000); Thomas Dee and Helen Fu, "Do Charter Schools Skim Students or Drain Resources?" *Economics of Education Review* 23, no. 3 (2004): 259–271; Amy S. Wells, et al., "Charter Schools and Racial and Social Class Segregation: Yet Another Sorting Machine?" in *A Nation at Risk: Preserving Education as an Engine for Social Mobility,* ed. Richard Kahlenberg (New York: Century Foundation Press, 2000), 169–222. For studies of charter school enrollments of "harder to serve" student populations (e.g., English language learners and students requiring special education services), see Jack Buckley and Carolyn Sattin-Bajaj, "Are ELL Students Underrepresented in Char-

ter Schools? Demographic Trends in New York City, 2006–2008," *Journal of School Choice* 5, no. 1 (2011): 1–26; Jack Buckley and Mark Schneider, "Are Charter School Students Harder to Educate? Evidence from Washington, D.C.," *Educational Evaluation and Policy Analysis* 27, no. 4 (2005): 365–380. For research on the impact of choice on school segregation, see Robert Bifulco and Helen F. Ladd, "School Choice, Racial Segregation, and Test-Score Gaps: Evidence from North Carolina's Charter School Program," *Journal of Policy Analysis and Management* 26, no. 1 (2007): 31–56; Kevin Booker, Ron Zimmer, and Richard Buddin, "The Effects of Charter Schools on School Peer Composition," Working paper WR-306-EDU (Santa Monica, CA: Rand Corporation, 2005); Ron Zimmer et al., "Charter Schools: Do They Cream Skim, Increase Segregation?" in *School Choice and School Improvement*, ed. Mark Berends, Marisa Cannata, and Ellen B. Goldring (Cambridge, MA: Harvard Education Press, 2011), 215–232. For analyses of the impact of increased competition from school choice on student achievement in traditional public schools, see Julian R. Betts, "The Competitive Effects of Charter Schools on Traditional Public Schools," in *Handbook of Research on School Choice*, ed. Mark Berends, Matthew G. Springer, Dale Ballou, and Herbert J. Walberg (New York: Routledge, 2009), 209–226.; Bifulco and Ladd, "School Choice," 2007; Caroline M. Hoxby, "School Choice and School Productivity: Could School Choice Be a Tide That Lifts All Boats?" in *Economics of School Choice*, ed. Caroline M. Hoxby (Chicago: University of Chicago Press, 2003), 287–341. Clive R. Belfield and Henry M. Levin, "The Effects of Competition on Educational Outcomes: A Review of U.S. Evidence," (New York: National Center for the Study of the Privatization of Education, Teachers College, Columbia University, 2002); Anna J. Egalite, "Measuring Competitive Effects From School Voucher Programs: A Systematic Review," *Journal of School Choice*, 7 no.4 (2013): 443–464; Cecilia E. Rouse, Jane Hannaway, Dan Goldhaber, and David N. Figlio, "Feeling the Florida Heat? How Low-Performing Schools Respond to Voucher and Accountability Pressure," *American Economic Journal: Economic Policy* 5, no. 2 (May 2013): 251–81; For research on whether choice improves operational and fiscal efficiency of traditional public schools, see David Arsen and Youngmei Ni, "Shaking up Public Schools with Competition: Are They Changing the Way They Spend Money?" in *School Choice and School Improvement*, ed. Mark Berends, Marisa Cannata, and Ellen B. Goldring (Cambridge, MA: Harvard Education Press, 2011), 193–213; Hoxby, *Economics*, 2003; Youngmei Ni, "Do Traditional Public Schools Benefit from Charter School Competition?" *Economics of Education Review* 28, no. 5 (2009): 571–584. For research on how choice impacts the resources available to students in traditional public schools, see Arsen and Ni, "Shaking Up," 2011; Dee and Fu, *Do Charter Schools Skim*, 2004; Amy S. Wells, "Why Public Policy Fails to Live up to the Potential of Charter School Reform: An Introduction," in *Where Charter School Policy Fails: The Problems of Accountability and Equity*, ed. Amy S. Wells (New York: Teachers College Press, 2002), 1–28; Bruce D. Baker, Ken Libby, and Kathryn Wi, *Spending by the Major Charter Management Organizations: Comparing Charter School and Local Public District Financial Resources* (Boulder, CO: National Education Policy Center, 2012. For comparisons of student achievement in schools of choice and traditional public schools, see Buckley and Schneider, "Charter School Students," 2005; Center for Research on Education

Outcomes, *Multiple Choice: Charter School Performance in 16 States* (Stanford, CA: Center for Research on Education Outcomes, 2009); Center for Research on Education Outcomes, *National Charter School Study* (Stanford, CA: Center for Research on Education Outcomes, 2013); Julie B. Cullen, Brian A. Jacob, and Steven Levitt, "The Impact of School Choice on Student Outcomes: An Analysis of the Chicago Public Schools," *Journal of Public Economics* 89, nos. 5–6 (2005): 729–760.; Caroline M. Hoxby and Sonali Murarka, "Charter Schools in New York City: Who Enrolls and How They Affect Their Students' Achievement," *NBER Working Paper 14852* (Cambridge, MA: National Bureau of Economic Research, 2009); Patrick J. Wolf et al., "School Vouchers in the Nation's Capital: Summary of Experimental Impacts," in *School Choice and School Improvement*, ed. Mark Berends, Marisa Cannata, and Ellen B. Goldring (Cambridge, MA: Harvard Education Press, 2011), 17–33.

11. Gary Orfield and Erica Frankenberg and Associates, *Educational Delusions? Why Choice Can Deepen Inequality and How to Make Schools Fair* (Berkeley, CA: University of California Press, 2013); Norman M. Fructer et al., *Is Demography Still Destiny? Neighborhood Demographics and Public High School Students' Readiness for College in New York City* (Providence, R.I.: Annenberg Institute for School Reform, Brown University, 2012); Lori Nathanson, Sean Corcoran, and Christine Baker-Smith, *High School Choice in NYC: A Report on the School Choices and Placements of Low-Achieving Students* (New York: The Research Alliance for New York City Schools & The Institute for Education and Social Policy, New York University, 2013); Sean P. Corcoran and Henry M. Levin, "School Choice and Competition in New York City Schools," in *Education Reform in New York City: Ambitious Change in the Nation's Most Complex School System*, ed. Jennifer A. O'Day, Catherine S. Bitter, and Louis M. Gomez (Cambridge, MA: Harvard Education Press, 2011), 199–224; Allison Roda and Amy S. Wells, "School Choice Policies and Racial Segregation: Where White Parents' Good Intentions, Anxiety and Privilege Collide," *American Journal of Education* 119, no. 2 (2013): 261–293.

12. Gary Orfield, John Kucsera, and Genevieve Siegel-Hawley, *E Pluribus . . . Separation: Deepening Double Segregation for More Students* (Los Angeles, CA: Civil Rights Project / Proyecto Derechos Civiles, 2012).

13. Thomas Stewart and Patrick J. Wolf explore and answer similar questions about families' experiences with school choice in their forthcoming book, *The School Choice Journey: School Vouchers and the Empowerment of Urban Families* (New York: Palgrave MacMillan, forthcoming). In it, they present the results of their study of 110 families participating in the District of Columbia's Opportunity Scholarship Program (OSP), a school voucher program, and they describe differing degrees of "empowerment" among parents in terms of their behaviors and relationships with schools.

CHAPTER 1

1. New York City Department of Planning, "Population Facts," www.nyc.gov/html/dcp/html/census/pop_facts.shtml (accessed September 10, 2013).

2. A Friedrich Heckmann and Dominique Schnapper, introduction to *The Integration of Immigrants in European Societies: National Differences and Trends of Convergence*, ed. Friedrich Heckmann and Dominique Schnapper (Stuttgart, Germany:

Lucius & Lucius, 2003), 9–14; Marcelo M. Suárez-Orozco, Carola Suárez-Orozco, and Carolyn Sattin-Bajaj, "Making Migration Work," *Peabody Journal of Education* 85, no. 4 (2010): 535–551; Bertelsmann Stiftung, (Eds.), *Immigrant students can succeed: Lessons from around the globe* (Gutersloh, Germany: Verlag Bertelsmann Stiftung, 2008).

3. U.S. Census Bureau, 2009 American Community Survey, *New York City, New York ACS Demographic and Housing Estimates: 2009*, www.nyc.gov/html/dcp/pdf/census/nyc_boro_demo_06to09_acs.pdf (accessed August 12, 2012).

4. Sam Roberts, "Listening to (and Saving) the World's Languages," *New York Times*, April 29, 2010, N.Y./Region section, New York edition; U.S. Census Bureau, *New York City, New York ACS Demographic.*

5. For a longer discussion of the income and educational diversity of the most recent waves of immigrants, see Marcelo M. Suárez-Orozco, "Right Moves? Immigration, Globalization, Utopia, and Dystopia," in *The New Immigration: An Interdisciplinary Reader*, ed. Marcelo M. Suarez-Orozco, Carola Suárez-Orozco, and Desirée B. Qin (New York: Routledge, 2005), 3–19.

6. Cited in Jeanne Batalova and Michael Fix, "College-Educated Immigrant Workers in the United States," *Migration Policy Institute*, www.migrationinformation.org/usfocus/display.cfm?ID=702#3 (accessed January 10, 2011).

7. Cited in Sam Roberts, "Census Shows How Recession Hit N.Y.," *New York Times*, September 29, 2010, N.Y./Region section, New York edition.

8. U.S. Census Bureau, *New York City, New York ACS Demographic.*

9. New York City Department of Education, *Comprehensive Education Plan (CEP) Schools Demographic Snapshot, 2006–2009*, http://schools.nyc.gov/Accountability/data/default.htm (accessed December 16, 2010).

10. New York City Department of Education, *New York City's English Language Learners: Demographics* (New York: Office of English Language Learners, 2008).

11. Norman M. Fructer et al., *Is Demography Still Destiny? Neighborhood Demographics and Public High School Students' Readiness for College in New York City* (Providence, R.I.: Annenberg Institute for School Reform, Brown University, 2012).

12. Madeline E. Lopez, "New York, Puerto Ricans, and the Dilemmas of Integration," in *From Grassroots to the Supreme Court: Brown v. Board of Education and American Democracy*, ed. Peter F. Lau (Durham, NC: Duke University Press, 2004), 300–320; Diane Ravitch, *The Great School Wars: A History of the New York City Public Schools* (Baltimore, MD: Johns Hopkins University Press, 1974).

13. Joel I. Klein et al., "How to Fix Our Schools: A Manifesto by Joel Klein, Michelle Rhee and Other Education Leaders," *Washington Post*, October 10, 2010, Opinion; Joe Nocera, "Lesson Plans from a Departing Schools Chief," *New York Times*, November 12, 2010, Business section, New York edition.

14. Ati' La Abdulkadiroglu, Parag A. Pathak, and Alvin E. Roth, "Practical Market Design: Four Matches, the New York City High School Match," *American Economic Review* 95, no. 2 (2005): 364–367.

15. Clara Hemphill and Kim Nauer, *The New Marketplace: How Small-School Reforms and School Choice Have Shaped New York City's High Schools* (New York: Center for New York City Affairs, The New School, 2009).

16. Ibid.

17. Ibid.

18. In a recent report on school choice in New York City for the Brown Center on Education Policy at Brookings, Grover (Russ) Whitehurst and Sara Whitfield argued that including all charter schools and interested private schools in the application process would improve the choice process and competition among schools (2).

19. Floyd Hammack, "Paths to Legislation or Litigation for Educational Privilege: New York and San Francisco Compared," *American Journal of Education* 116, no. 3 (2010): 371–395.

20. NAACP Legal Defense and Education Fund, "Case: New York City Specialized High School Complaint," NAACP-LDF, www.naacpldf.org/case-issue/new-york-city -specialized-high-school-complaint (accessed 10 August, 2013); Al Baker, "Girls Excel in the Classroom but Lag in Entry to Eight Elite Schools in the City," *New York Times*, March 23, 2013, N.Y./Region, New York edition.

21. Fructer et al., *Is Demography Still Destiny?*

22. Sean P. Corcoran and Henry M. Levin, "School Choice and Competition in New York City Schools," in *Education Reform in New York City: Ambitious Change in the Nation's Most Complex School System*, ed. Jennifer A. O'Day, Catherine S. Bitter, and Louis M. Gomez (Cambridge, MA: Harvard Education Press, 2011), 199–224.

23. New York City Department of Education, "For Eighth Straight Year, More Than 80 Percent of Students Are Admitted to One of Their Top High School Choices," NYCDOE, http://schools.nyc.gov/Offices/mediarelations/NewsandSpeeches/2012-2013/ 031513_eightstraightyear.htm (accessed April 10, 2013).

24. Corcoran and Levin, "School Choice," 2011; Fructer, et al., *Is Demography Still Destiny?*, 2012; Hemphill and Nauer, *New Marketplace*, 2009.

25. Lori Nathanson, Sean Corcoran, and Christine Baker-Smith, *High School Choice in NYC: A Report on the School Choices and Placements of Low-Achieving Students* (New York: The Research Alliance for New York City Schools and the Institute for Education and Social Policy, New York University, 2013).

26. G. Russ Whitehurst and Sarah Whitfield, *School Choice and School Performance in New York City Public Schools: Will the Past Be Prologue?* (Washington, DC: Brown Center on Education Policy at Brookings, 2013); U.S. Department of Education, National Center for Education Statistics, *The Nation's Report Card: Reading 2011*, NCES 2012-457 (Washington, DC: Government Printing Office, 2012).

27. U.S. Department of Labor, Bureau of Labor Statistics, 2010, www.bls.gov/cps/ cpsa2009.pdf (accessed March 4, 2010).; Henry M. Levin and Clive R. Belfield, "Educational Interventions to Raise High School Graduation Rates," in *The Price We Pay: Economic and Social Consequences of Inadequate Education*, ed. Clive R. Belfield and Henry M. Levin (Washington, DC: Brookings Institution Press, 2007), 177–199; J. R. Pleis, B. W. Ward, and J. W. Lucas, *Vital and Health Statistics: Summary Health Statistics for U.S. Adults: National Health Interview Survey, 2009*, U.S. Department of Health and Human Services, Centers for Disease Control and Prevention, National Center for Health Statistics series 10, no. 249. (Hyattsville, MD: National Center for Health Statistics, 2010).

28. Hemphill and Nauer, *New Marketplace*.

29. Benjamin Meade et al., *Making the Grade in New York City Schools: Progress Report Grades and Black and Latino Students* (New York: The Metropolitan Center for Urban Education, Steinhardt School of Culture, Education and Human Development, New York University, 2009).

30. Corcoran and Levin, *School Choice.*

31. New York City Department of Education, *New York City Graduation Rates Class of 2011 (2007 Cohort)*, www.nyc.gov/html/om/pdf/2012/2011_grad_deck _presentation.pdf (accessed March 15, 2013).

32. Fructer et al., *Is Demography Still Destiny?*

33. Ibid.

34. Ibid., 2.

CHAPTER 2

1. New York City Department of Education, "Admissions Process," http://schools .nyc.gov/ChoicesEnrollment/High/Admissions (accessed September 16, 2013).

2. U.S. Bureau of the Census, *Statistical Abstract of the United States: Adult Computer and Adult Internet Users by Selected Characteristics: 2000 to 2011*, www .census.gov/compendia/statab/2012/tables/12s1158.pdf (accessed March 1, 2012); Kathryn Zickuhr and Aaron Smith, *Digital Differences* (Washington, DC: Pew Research Center's Internet & American Life Project, 2012).

3. The newest version of the directory (for the 2013–14 school year) includes an entire section labeled "accountability data" on each school's page. This table contains the school's overall *Progress Report* grade and grades from 2011 and 2012 broken down by subcategories (student progress, student performance, school environment, and college and career readiness), the graduation rate and postsecondary enrollment rate, and its quality review score from 2009.

4. Concha Delgado-Gaitan, "School Matters in the Mexican-American Home: Socializing Children to Education," *American Educational Research Journal* 29, no. 3 (1992): 495–513; Annette Lareau, *Unequal Childhoods: Class, Race, and Family Life* (Berkeley, CA: University of California Press, 2003); Leslie Reese et al., "The Concept of *Educación*: Latino Families and American Schooling," *International Journal of Educational Research* 23, no. 1 (1995): 57–81.

5. Geoff Decker, G, "Above the Fray, Students in Foster Care Get High School Fair Help," *Gotham Schools.* http://ny.chalkbeat.org/2012/10/02/above-the-fray-students -in-foster-care-get-high-school-fair-help/ (accessed March 15, 2013).

6. John E. Chubb and Terry M. Moe, *Politics, Markets, and America's Schools* (Washington, DC: Brookings Institution, 1990).

7. Chubb and Moe, *Politics,* 564.

CHAPTER 3

1. Melissa Roderick, "School Transitions and School Dropout," in *Advances in Educational Policy*, ed. Kenneth Wong (Greenwich, CT: JAI Press, 1994), 135–185.

2. Clara Hemphill and Kim Nauer, *The New Marketplace: How Small-School Reforms and School Choice Have Shaped New York City's High Schools* (New York: Center for New York City Affairs, the New School, 2009).

3. Hemphill and Nauer, *New Marketplace*; New York City Department of Education, "For Eighth Straight Year, More Than 80 Percent of Students Are Admitted to One of Their Top High School Choices," http://schools.nyc.gov/Offices/mediarelations/NewsandSpeeches/2012-2013/031513_eightstraightyear.htm (accessed April 10, 2013).

4. Jennifer Booher-Jennings, "Below the Bubble: 'Educational Triage' and the Texas Accountability System," *American Educational Research Journal* 42, no. 2 (2005): 231–268; David N. Figlio and Lawrence S. Getzler, "Accountability, Ability and Disability: Gaming the System?" in *Improving School Accountability: Advances in Applied Microeconomics*, vol. 14 (Bingley, U.K: Emerald Group Publishing, 2006), 35–49; Derek Neal and Diane W. Schanzenbach, "Left Behind by Design: Proficiency Counts and Test-based Accountability," *Review of Economics and Statistics* 92, no. 2 (2007): 263–283.

CHAPTER 4

1. While academic track appeared to be the most powerful grouping variable, the differences observed might also be understood as a function of students' racial/ethnic origin, class, and cultural backgrounds. All but one of the gifted and talented-track students interviewed were second-generation children of Chinese and South Asian immigrants. This reflected the demographic composition of the gifted and talented track, where nearly 84 percent of students were first- or second-generation children of East or South Asian immigrants. Consonant with the larger student-body makeup, the rest of the students in the interview sample were first- and second-generation children of Latin American immigrants or African American or third-generation or higher students. Because this study was not designed to isolate the effects of academic track versus cultural/ethnic factors in determining students' school choice behaviors, no definitive conclusions were reached regarding the source of the differences observed. However, the varying salience of track/student academic level versus racial/ethnic background and immigrant origins has been analyzed and discussed when applicable.

2. For research on the impact of peers on students' school adjustment, see Thomas J. Berndt and Keunho Keefe, "Friends' Influence on Adolescents' Adjustment to School," *Child Development* 66, no. 5 (1995): 1312–1329; on motivation, see Jacquelynne S. Eccles, Allan Wigfield, and Ulrich Schiefele, "Motivation to Succeed," in *Social, Emotional and Personality Development*, vol. 3 of *Handbook of Child Psychology*, ed. Nancy Eisenberg (New York: Wiley, 1998), 1017–1094; on academic achievement, see Robert Crosnoe and Belinda Needham, "Holism, Contextual Variability, and the Study of Friendships in Adolescent Development," *Child Development* 75, no. 1 (2004): 264–279; Robert K. Ream and Russell W. Rumberger, "Student Engagement, Peer Social Capital, and School Dropout among Mexican American and Non-Latino White Students," *Sociology of Education* 81, no. 2 (2008): 109–139; for positive and negative peer influences, see Andrew Fuligni et al., "Early Adolescent Peer Orientation and Adjustment During High School," *Developmental Psychology* 37, no. 1 (2001): 28–36; Alejandro Portes and Patricia Landolt, "The Downside of Social Capital," *American Prospect* 26 (1996): 18–21; Robert K. Ream, "Counterfeit Social Capital and Mexican American Underachievement," *Education Evaluation and Policy Analysis* 25, no. 3 (2003): 237–262.

3. All high schools have been given pseudonyms.

4. For some examples of research on parents' use of choice materials, see Mark Schneider, Paul Teske, and Melissa Marschall, *Choosing Schools: Consumer Choice and the Quality of American Schools* (Princeton, NJ: Princeton University Press, 2000); Paul Teske, Jodi Fitzpatrick, and Gabriel Kaplan, *Opening Doors: Low-Income Parents Search for the Right School* (Seattle, WA: Center on Reinventing Public Education, University of Washington, 2007); Jack Buckley and Mark Schneider, *Charter Schools: Hope or Hype?* (Princeton, NJ: Princeton University Press, 2007); Justine Hastings, Richard Van Weelden, and Jeffrey M. Weinstein, "Preferences, Information, and Parental Choice Behavior in Public School Choice," *NBER Working Paper no. 12995* (Cambridge, MA: National Bureau of Economic Research, 2007); Lois Andre-Bechely, *Could It Be Otherwise? Parents and the Inequities of Public School Choice* (New York: Routledge, 2005).

5. David J. Armour and Brett M. Peiser, "Interdistrict Choice in Massachusetts," in *Learning from School Choice*, ed. Paul E. Peterson and Bryan C. Hassel (Washington, DC: Brookings Institution, 1998), 157–186; Buckley & Schneider, *Charter Schools: Hope or Hype?*; Laura S. Hamilton and Kacey Guin, "Understanding How Families Choose Schools," in *Getting Choice Right: Ensuring Equity and Efficiency in Education Policy*, ed. Julian R. Betts and Tom Loveless (Washington, DC: Brookings Institution Press, 2005), 40–60; Valerie J. Martinez, R. Kenneth Godwin, and Frank R. Kemerer, "Public School Choice in San Antonio: Who Chooses and with What Effects?," in *Who Chooses? Who Loses? Culture, Institutions, and the Unequal Effects of School Choice*, ed. Bruce Fuller and Richard F. Elmore (New York: Teachers College Press, 1996), 50–69; Schneider, Teske, and Marschall, *Choosing Schools*.

6. For an exception, see Valerie E. Lee and Douglas D. Ready, *Schools Within Schools: Possibilities and Pitfalls of High School Reform* (New York: Teachers College Press, 2007).

7. Concha Delgado-Gaitan, "School Matters in the Mexican-American Home: Socializing Children to Education," *American Educational Research Journal* 29 no. 3 (1992): 495–513; Leslie Reese et al., "The Concept of *Educación*: Latino Families and American Schooling," *International Journal of Educational Research* 23, no. 1 (1995): 57–81; Guadalupe Valdes, *Con Respeto: Bridging the Distance between Culturally Diverse Families and Schools: An Ethnographic Portrait* (New York: Teachers College Press, 1996).

8. Delgado-Gaitan, *School Matters*; Reese et al., *Educación*; Valdes, *Con Respeto*.

9. Reese et al., "The Concept of *Educación*"; Valdes, *Con Respeto*.

10. Robert A. LeVine and Merry I. White, *Human Conditions: The Cultural Basis of Educational Development* (New York: Routledge, 1986); Erich Rueschenberg and Raymond Buriel, "Latino Family Functioning and Acculturation: A Family Systems Perspective," *Hispanic Journal of Behavioral Sciences* 11, no. 3 (1989): 232–244.

11. Lori Nathanson, Sean Corcoran, and Christine Baker-Smith, *High School Choice in NYC: A Report on the School Choices and Placements of Low-Achieving Students* (New York: The Research Alliance for New York City Schools and the Institute for Education and Social Policy, New York University, 2013).

12. Clara Hemphill and Kim Nauer, *The New Marketplace: How Small-School Reforms and School Choice Have Shaped New York City's High Schools* (New York: Center for New York City Affairs, the New School, 2009).

CHAPTER 5

1. Campaign for Fiscal Equity, *Diploma Dilemma: Rising Standards, the Regents Diploma, and Schools That Beat the Odds*, report prepared by the Campaign for Fiscal Equity, September 2010; cited in Norman M. Fructer et al., *Is Demography Still Destiny? Neighborhood Demographics and Public High School Students' Readiness for College in New York City* (Providence, RI: Annenberg Institute for School Reform, Brown University, 2012).

2. Lawrence F. Katz and Claudia Goldin, *The Race Between Education and Technology* (Cambridge, MA: Harvard University Press, 2008); U.S. Department of Labor, Bureau of Labor Statistics, *Employment and Earnings January 2010*, www.bls.gov/cps/cpsa2009.pdf (accessed March 4, 2010); Thomas D. Snyder and Sally A. Dillow, *Digest of Education Statistics, 2010*, National Center for Education Statistics, U.S. Department of Education, NCES 2011-015 (Washington, DC: Government Printing Office, 2011).

3. Pierre Bourdieu, *Outline of a Theory of Practice* (Cambridge, UK: Cambridge University Press, 1977).

4. Stephen J. Ball, "Education Markets, Choice, and Social Class: The Market as a Class Strategy in the UK and the USA," *British Journal of Sociology of Education* 14, no. 1 (1993): 3–19; Paul DiMaggio, "Review Essay on Pierre Bourdieu," *American Journal of Sociology* 84, no. 6 (1979): 1460–1474; Gregory J. Duncan and Katherine Magnuson, "The Nature and Impact of Early Achievement Skills, Attention Skills, and Behavior Problems," in *Whither Opportunity? Rising Inequality, Schools, and Children's Life Chances*, ed. Gregory J. Duncan and Richard J. Murnane (New York: Russell Sage Foundation, 2011), 47–70; Michèle Lamont and Annette Lareau, "Cultural Capital: Allusions, Gaps, and Glissandos in Recent Theoretical Developments," *Sociological Theory* 6, no. 2 (1988): 153–168; Annette Lareau, *Unequal Childhoods: Class, Race, and Family Life* (Berkeley, CA: University of California Press, 2003); Jay MacLeod, *Ain't No Making It: Aspirations and Attainment in a Low-Income Neighborhood* (Boulder, CO: Westview Press, 1995); Claire Smrekar and Ellen Goldring, *School Choice in Urban America: Magnet Schools and the Pursuit of Equity* (New York: Teachers College Press, 1999); Amy S. Wells, "Why Public Policy Fails to Live up to the Potential of Charter School Reform: An Introduction," in *Where Charter School Policy Fails: The Problems of Accountability and Equity*, ed. Amy S. Wells (New York: Teachers College Press, 2002), 1–28.

5. Uri Brofenbrenner, *The Ecology of Human Development: Experiments by Nature and Design* (Cambridge, MA: Harvard University Press, 1979).

6. Bourdieu used the notion of habitus, or "a matrix of perceptions, appreciations, and actions," to understand the interrelationship between individual agency and social classification (*Outline* 83). Habitus has also been used to analyze individual and group-level practices and to disentangle mechanisms of social reproduction (Mac-

Leod, *Aspirations*; Diane Reay, "'They Employ Cleaners to Do That': Habitus in the Primary Classroom," *British Journal of Sociology of Education* 16, no. 3 (1995): 353–371. It relates to the concepts of an *institutional compass* and a *multiply reinforced orientation* in that the gifted and talented students' successful development of each of them depended on the possession of certain values and beliefs associated with effective school search strategies.

7. Robert J. Sampson, Stephen W. Raudenbush, and Felton Earls, "Neighborhoods and Violent Crime: A Multilevel Study of Collective Efficacy," *Science* 277 (1997): 918–924.

8. James Coleman, "Social Capital in the Creation of Human Capital," *American Journal of Sociology* 94 (1998): S95–S120.

9. Coleman, "Social Capital," S106.

10. William G. Bowen, Matthew M. Chingos, and Michael S. McPherson, *Crossing the Finish Line: Completing College at America's Public Universities* (Princeton, NJ: Princeton University Press, 2009); Caroline M. Hoxby and Christopher Avery, "The Missing 'One-Offs': The Hidden Supply of High-Achieving, Low Income Students," *NBER Working Paper no. 18586* (Cambridge, MA: National Bureau of Economic Research, 2012); Melissa Roderick, Vanessa Coca, and Jenny Nagaoka, "Potholes on the Road to College: High School Effects in Shaping Urban Students' Participation in College Application, Four-Year College Enrollment and College Match," *Sociology of Education* 84, no. 3 (2011): 178–211; Jonathan Smith et al., *Getting into College: Postsecondary Academic Undermatch* (Washington, DC: The College Board Advocacy & Policy Center, 2012).

11. Snyder and Dillow, *Digest of Education Statistics, 2010.*

12. Robert Levine, Sarah Levine, and Beatrice Schnell, "Improve the Women: Mass Schooling, Female Literacy and Worldwide Social Change," *Harvard Educational Review* 71, no. 1 (2001): 21.

13. Levine, Levine, and Schnell, "Improve the Women," 22.

14. Carola Suárez-Orozco, Marcelo M. Suárez-Orozco, and Irina Todorova, *Learning a New Land: Immigrant Students in American Society* (Cambridge, MA: Belknap Press of Harvard University, 2008).

15. Lois Andre-Bechely, *Could It Be Otherwise? Parents and the Inequities of Public School Choice* (New York: Routledge, 2005); Paul T. Hill, ed., *Choice with Equity* (Stanford, CA: Hoover Institution Press, 2002); Lareau, *Unequal Childhoods*; Mark Schneider, Paul Teske, and Melissa Marschall, *Choosing Schools: Consumer Choice and the Quality of American Schools* (Princeton, NJ: Princeton University Press, 2000); Ricardo D. Stanton-Salazar, *Manufacturing Hope and Despair: The School and Kin Support Networks of U.S.-Mexican Youth* (New York: Teachers College Press, 2001); Paul Teske, Mark Schneider, Christine Roch, and Melissa Marschall, "Public School Choice: A Status Report," in *City Schools: Lessons from New York City*, ed. Diane Ravitch (Baltimore: Johns Hopkins University Press, 2000), 313–365; Paul Teske, Jodi Fitzpatrick, and Gabriel Kaplan, *Opening Doors: Low-Income Parents Search for the Right School* (Seattle, WA: Center on Reinventing Public Education, University of Washington, 2007).

16. Stanton-Salazar, *Manufacturing Hope*, 251.
17. Ibid., 21.
18. Ibid., 247.

CHAPTER 6

1. See methodological appendix for parent interview sample.

2. Stephen J. Ball, "Education Markets, Choice, and Social Class: The Market as a Class Strategy in the UK and the USA," *British Journal of Sociology of Education* 14, no. 1 (1993); Ellen Brantlinger, *Dividing Classes: How the Middle Class Negotiates and Rationalizes School Advantage* (New York: Routledge Falmer, 2003); Diane Reay, "'They Employ Cleaners to Do That': Habitus in the Primary Classroom," *British Journal of Sociology of Education* 16, no. 3 (1995): 353–371; Claire Smrekar and Ellen Goldring, *School Choice in Urban America: Magnet Schools and the Pursuit of Equity* (New York: Teachers College Press, 1999); Guadalupe Valdes, *Con Respeto: Bridging the Distance between Culturally Diverse Families and Schools: An Ethnographic Portrait* (New York: Teachers College Press, 1996).

3. Clara Hemphill et al., *New York City's Best Public High Schools in NYC: A Parent's Guide*, (New York: Teacher's College Press, 2007).

4. Concha Delgado-Gaitan, "School Matters in the Mexican-American Home: Socializing Children to Education," *American Educational Research Journal* 29, no. 3 (1992): 495–513; Leslie Reese et al., "The Concept of *Educación*: Latino Families and American Schooling," *International Journal of Educational Research* 23, no. 1 (1995): 57–81; Valdes, *Con Respeto*; Richard R. Valencia and Mary S. Black, "Mexican Americans Don't Value Education! On the Basis of the Myth, Mythmaking, and Debunking," *Journal of Latinos and Education* 1, no. 2 (2002): 81–103.

5. Delgado-Gaitan, "School Matters"; Reese et al., "The Concept of *Educación*"; Valdes, *Con Respeto*.

6. Reese et al., "The Concept of *Educación*," 67.

7. James Coleman, "Social Capital in the Creation of Human Capital," *American Journal of Sociology* 94 (1998): S95–S120.

8. Ricardo D. Stanton-Salazar, *Manufacturing Hope and Despair: The School and Kin Support Networks of U.S.-Mexican Youth* (New York: Teachers College Press, 2001).

9. Most studies of low-income Latin American immigrant parents have found that they tend to defer to teachers and school administrators on academic matters, which they believe to be outside of their realm of expertise and authority. Parents treat teachers as educated professionals who know best about academic matters and are better equipped to make academic decisions for their children while they view themselves as responsible for the moral education of a child at home. For more on this, see Delgado-Gaitan, "School Matters"; Stanton-Salazar, *Manufacturing Hope*; Carola Suárez-Orozco and Marcelo M. Suárez-Orozco, *Children of Immigration* (Cambridge, MA: Harvard University Press, 2001).

10. Suárez-Orozco and Suárez-Orozco, *Children of Immigration*; Min Zhou, "Growing up American: The Challenge Confronting Immigrant Children and Children of Immigrants," *Annual Review of Sociology* 23, no. 1 (1997): 63–95.

11. For categories of parent choosers, see Jeffrey Henig, "The Local Dynamics of Choice: Ethnic Preferences and Institutional Responses," in *Who Chooses? Who Loses? Culture, Institutions, and the Unequal Effects of School Choice*, ed. Bruce Fuller and Richard F. Elmore (New York: Teachers College Press, 1996), 95–117; Mark Schneider, Paul Teske, and Melissa Marschall, *Choosing Schools: Consumer Choice and the Quality of American Schools* (Princeton, NJ: Princeton University Press, 2000); Jack Buckley and Mark Schneider, *Charter Schools: Hope or Hype?* (Princeton, NJ: Princeton University Press, 2007).

12. For other studies of how middle-class parents preserve educational privileges, see Brantlinger, *Dividing Classes*; Maia B. Cucchiara and Erin M. Horvat, "Perils and Promises: Middle-Class Parental Involvement in Urban Schools," *American Educational Research Journal* 46, no. 4 (2009): 974–1004; Erin M. Horvat, Elliot B. Weininger, and Annette Lareau, "From Social Ties to Social Capital: Class Differences in the Relation between School and Parent Networks," *American Educational Research Journal* 40, no. 2 (2003): 319–351; Annette Lareau, *Unequal Childhoods: Class, Race, and Family Life* (Berkeley: University of California Press, 2003); Mitchell L. Stevens, *Creating a Class: College Admissions and the Education of Elites* (Cambridge, MA: Harvard University Press, 2007); Amy S. Wells and Allison Roda, "White Parents, Diversity, and School Choice Policies: Where Good Intentions, Anxiety, and Privilege Collide," *American Journal of Education* 119, no. 2 (2013): 261–293.

13. John E. Chubb and Terry M. Moe, *Politics, Markets, and America's Schools* (Washington, DC: Brookings Institution, 1990).

14. Ball, "Education Markets"; Brantlinger, *Dividing Classes*; Lisa Delpit, *Other People's Children: Cultural Conflict in the Classroom* (New York: The New Press, 1995); Bruce Fuller, *Standardized Childhood: The Political and Cultural Struggle Over Early Education* (Stanford, CA: Stanford University Press, 2007); Reay, "'They Employ Cleaners'"; Smrekar and Goldring, *School Choice*; Valdes, *Con Respeto*.

15. For examples of increased alienation, see Brantlinger, *Dividing Classes*; John U. Ogbu, "Minority Coping Responses and School Experience," *Journal of Psychohistory* 18, no. 4 (1991): 433–456; John U. Ogbu, *Black American Students in an Affluent Suburb: A Study of Academic Disengagement* (Mahwah, NJ: Lawrence Erlbaum Associates, 2003); Paul Willis, *Learning to Labor: How Working Class Kids Get Working Class Jobs* (New York: Columbia University Press, 1977); for research on delayed academic progress, see Shirley B. Heath, *Ways with Words: Language, Life, and Work in Communities and Classrooms* (Cambridge, UK: Cambridge University Press, 1983); Delpit, *Other People's Children*; for work on the construction of social-deficit ideas, see Valencia and Black, "Mexican Americans"; for a discussion of social and cultural stratification, see Michael Apple, *Education and Power* (Boston, MA: Routledge & Kegan Paul, 1982); Pierre Bourdieu, "Cultural Reproduction and Social Reproduction," in *Power and Ideology in Education*, ed. Jerome Karabel & A. H. Halsey (New York: Oxford University Press, 1977), 487–511; Samuel Bowles and Herbert Gintis, *Schooling in Capitalist America: Educational Reform and the Contradictions of Economic Life* (New York: Basic Books, 1976); and Martin Carnoy and Henry M. Levin, *Schooling and Work in the Democratic State* (Stanford, CA: Stanford University Press, 1985).

16. William S. Koski and Rob Reich, "When 'Adequate' Isn't: The Retreat from Equity in Educational Law and Policy and Why It Matters," *Emory Law Journal* 26, no. 3 (2006): 547.

17. Martha J. Bailey and Susan Dynarski, "Inequality in Postsecondary Education," in *Whither Opportunity? Rising Inequality, Schools, and Children's Life Chances*, ed. Gregory J. Duncan and Richard J. Murnane (New York: Russell Sage Foundation, 2011), 117–131; Julie R. Posselt, Ozan Jaquette, Rob Bielby, and Michael N. Bastedo, "Access Without Equity: Longitudinal Analyses of Institutional Stratification by Race and Ethnicity, 1972–2004," *American Educational Research Journal* 49, no. 6 (2012): 1074–1111; Andrew Kelly, Mark Schneider, and Kevin Carey, *Rising to the Challenge: Hispanic College Graduation Rates as a National Priority* (Washington, DC: American Enterprise Institute, 2010); Thomas D. Snyder and Sally A. Dillow, *Digest of Education Statistics, 2010*, U.S. Department of Education, National Center for Education Statistics, NCES 2011-015 (Washington, DC: Government Printing Office, 2011).

18. Koski and Reich, "When 'Adequate' Isn't," 547.

19. Koski and Reich, "When 'Adequate' Isn't"; Brantlinger, *Dividing Classes*; Bruce Fuller and Richard F. Elmore, eds., *Who Chooses? Who Loses? Culture, Institutions, and the Unequal Effects of School Choice* (New York: Teachers College Press, 1996); Amy S. Wells, "Why Public Policy Fails to Live up to the Potential of Charter School Reform: An Introduction," in *Where Charter School Policy Fails: The Problems of Accountability and Equity*, ed. Amy S. Wells (New York: Teachers College Press, 2002), 1–28.

20. Stephen J. Ball, Richard Bowe, and Sharon Gerwitz, "Circuits of Schooling: A Sociological Exploration of Parental Choice of School in Social Class Contexts," *Sociological Review* 43 no. 1, 52–78.

CONCLUSION

1. Martin Forsey, Scott Davies, and Geoffrey Walford, eds., *The Globalisation of School Choice?* (Oxford, England: Symposium Books, Oxford Studies in Comparative Education, 2008); David N. Plank and Gary Sykes, eds., *Choosing Choice: School Choice in International Perspective* (New York: Teachers College Press, 2003).

2. John E. Chubb and Terry M. Moe, *Politics, Markets, and America's Schools* (Washington, DC: Brookings Institution, 1990); Milton Friedman, *Capitalism and Freedom* (Chicago: University of Chicago Press, 1962); William G. Howell and Paul E. Peterson, *The Education Gap: Vouchers and Urban Schools* (Washington, DC: Brookings Institution Press, 2006).

3. Edward Crowe, *Measuring What Matters: A Stronger Accountability Model for Teacher Education* (Washington: Center for American Progress, 2010); Edward Crowe, *Race to the Top and Teacher Preparation: Analyzing State Strategies for Ensuring Real Accountability and Fostering Program Innovation* (Washington: Center for American Progress, 2011).

4. Sammy Steen and Pedro Noguera, "A Broader, Bolder Approach to Education Reform: Expanded Partnership Roles for School Counselors," *Professional School Counseling* 14, no.1 (2010): 46.

5. A strong "college-going culture" that successfully promotes college awareness, preparation, and enrollment has been understood to include norms, behaviors, expectations, and support structures related to college preparation and enrollment. See Jeannie Oakes, Julie Mendoza, and David Silver, "California Opportunity Indicators: Information and Monitoring California's Progress Toward Equitable College Access," in *Expanding Opportunity in Higher Education: Leveraging Promise*, ed. Patricia Gándara and Gary Orfield (Albany: SUNY Press, 2006), 19–52; Melissa Roderick et al., *From High School to the Future: Potholes on the Road to College* (Chicago: University of Chicago, Consortium on Chicago School Research, 2008). It can instill in students an understanding of the potential value of college early on as well as "set norms for college attendance, provide information, relationships, and access to concrete support and expert knowledge to build bridges to the future" (Roderick et al., *From High School*, 7).

6. Researchers at the Chicago Consortium for Schools Research combined the percentage of prior graduates attending a four-year college with teachers' impressions of the school's "college climate" captured in a survey to determine college-going culture. Similarly, they measured a high school's organization around postsecondary planning based on the percentage of prior graduates who completed a Free Application for Federal Student Aid (FAFSA) and the percentage of prior graduates who applied to three or more postsecondary educational institutions (Roderick et al., *From High School*).

7. Roderick et al., *From High School*.

8. Concha Delgado-Gaitan, "Involving Parents in the Schools: A Process of Change for Involving Parents," *American Journal of Education* 100, no. 1 (1991): 20–46; Pedro A. Noguera, *City Schools and the American Dream: Reclaiming the Promise of Public Education* (New York: Teachers College Press, 2003); Lisa M. Stulberg, *Race, Schools and Hope: African Americans and School Choice after Brown* (New York: Teachers College Press, 2008).

9. Sylvia Hurtado, et al., "Differences in College Access and Choice among Racial/Ethnic Groups: Identifying Continuing Barriers," *Research in Higher Education*, 38, no. 1 (1997): 43–75.

10. Linda Levine, *The U.S. Income Distribution and Mobility: Trends and International Comparisons* (Washington, DC: Congressional Research Service Report 7-5700, 2012); Emmanuel Saez, "Striking It Richer: The Evolution of Top Incomes in the United States (Updated with 2011 Estimates)," http://elsa.berkeley.edu/~saez/saez-UStopincomes-2011.pdf (accessed March 3, 2013); Sean F. Reardon, "The Widening Achievement Gap between the Rich and the Poor: New Evidence and Possible Explanations," in *Whither Opportunity? Rising Inequality, Schools, and Children's Life Chances*, ed. Gregory J. Duncan and Richard J. Murnane (New York: Russell Sage Foundation, 2011), 91–116; Martha J. Bailey and Susan Dynarski, "Inequality in Postsecondary Education," in *Whither Opportunity?*, 117–131.

11. David Tyack, "Restructuring in Historical Perspective: Tinkering toward Utopia," *Teachers College Record* 92, no. 2 (1990): 170–191.

12. *Broader, Bolder Approach to Education*, www.boldapproach.org/bold_approach_full_statement.pdf (accessed January 20, 2011).

13. Ibid.

ACKNOWLEDGMENTS

This project would not have been possible without the guidance, support, cheerleading, and good humor of more people than there is room to thank. First and foremost I am indebted to the students, parents, and staff at IS 725 who so graciously welcomed me into their classrooms and their homes, their lunch tables and offices, and shared a small slice of their lives with me. I can think of no better compliment as an ethnographer than to be treated by school personnel as a colleague rather than an outsider, and the smiles, waves, and warm greetings from students made my daily two-hour commute well worth it. The honesty with which participants responded to my inquiries was critical to the insights developed through this research, and without their openness my understanding would have been much more limited.

The original dissertation research on which *Unaccompanied Minors* is based was a truly collaborative endeavor that began long before I embarked on the actual data collection. My advisor and mentor, Marcelo Suárez-Orozco, took me under his expansive wing and helped me find my way as a researcher and scholar of immigrant youth; his contributions to the study and book are too many to name. I am grateful for the support and guidance of Carola Suárez-Orozco, who showed me how it is possible to be a leading academic, invest in developing the next generation of researchers, and also be a kind and compassionate colleague, friend, mother, and wife. Pedro Noguera, Cynthia Miller-Idriss, Jack Buckley, Sean Corcoran, Floyd Hammack, and Jennifer Jennings at NYU were all instrumental in helping me see this project through to fruition. I am thankful for the guidance and wise counsel of Rick Hess during the early stages of the manuscript-development process.

My colleagues and students in the College of Education and Human Services at Seton Hall University welcomed me wholeheartedly to a wonderfully supportive and stimulating community, and they have been unflagging in their support of my work at every stage. I am especially thankful for the mentorship that Elaine Walker has provided since my first day on campus and for Kevin Iglesias's tireless assistance. I would not have gotten this manuscript done without the encouragement, pestering, and positive vibes sent by the UFO writing crew of Donovan Sherman, Marianne Lloyd, Kurt Rotthoff, Leslie Bunnage, and Anca Cotet. My editor at Harvard Education Press, Caroline Chauncey, has been a staunch advocate since the early stages of this work, and I am grateful for her enthusiasm for and deep investment in this project. She's been so much more than an editor and has made this experience truly a pleasure.

I am indebted to the friends and family members who have accompanied me on this journey for many years. Alisha Cipriano, Julie Jastremski, Leah Harsfield, Rebecca Koenig Berrebi, Lauren Vose, and Mara Brain have listened to me talk about this project for more years than I care to admit, and their own experiences as teachers, students, and parents informed my work. Monisha Bajaj has been a role model, mentor, and sounding board from day one, and I'm thankful for her support and that of Bikku Kuruvila, Asha Bajaj, and Dinesh Bajaj. Rhonda and Robert Sattin have nurtured my passions, encouraged my explorations, and always done everything in their power to help me succeed, and their impact as well as that of my siblings, Joanna and Ryan McConnell and James Sattin, is incalculable.

There are no words to describe all that Rajeev, my husband, is and everything he does to enrich my life and make even the most difficult task seem manageable. I am thankful every day for him and the joy, laughter, and kindness he brings everywhere he goes. This book is for Rajeev, Dylan, and Rafa.

ABOUT THE AUTHOR

CAROLYN SATTIN-BAJAJ is an assistant professor in the Department of Education Leadership, Management and Policy at Seton Hall University. Her research focuses on issues of educational equity and access for Latino, immigrant-origin students and families across the P–20 educational spectrum. Her work on school choice, immigrant students, and educational equity has appeared in a variety of academic journals and popular media outlets including the *Peabody Journal of Education, Journal of School Choice, The Huffington Post*, and the *Schoolbook* website. She is co-editor with Frederick M. Hess of *Rethinking School Systems: A Vision for Comprehensive Reform in Milwaukee and Beyond* (Rowman & Littlefield, 2013) and co-editor with Marcelo Suárez-Orozco of *Educating the Whole Child for the Whole World: The Ross School Model and Education for the Global Era* (New York University Press, 2010). Prior to earning her doctorate, she worked on secondary school reform at the New York City Department of Education. She lives in Montclair, New Jersey, with her husband and two sons.

INDEX